My Kind of People
My Kind of Cooking

EVELYN CURTIS

First Published in 2000 by Evelyn Curtis
Sunset House, 3 The Glebe, Lavenham, Suffolk CO10 9SN

ISBN 0-9539806-0-X

Photography by Michael Hodges, Lavenham Photographic,
3 Church Street, Lavenham, Suffolk.

Designed and printed by
The Lavenham Press, Lavenham, Suffolk CO10 9RN

This book is dedicated to my husband Cyril,
whose encouragement and patience never ceases to
amaze me, and whose wisdom echoes the words of
Matthew Prior (1667–1726)

'Be to her virtues very kind.
Be to her faults a little blind'.

Peanut biscuits and fudge

Acknowledgements

Writing another cookery book, even if it's one *'with a difference'*, has mostly been fun, but it hasn't always been easy, especially at the end, when I have had to meet deadlines. It's then that I have come to rely on the help and encouragement of the many people who have been involved with the production of this book.

First I must thank all the contributors, who so readily made themselves available to me at all times. To Anne Faiers who always came to my rescue when I needed something baked in a hurry for the photograph shoots, and to Kathleen Buckle, my thanks to you both.

To Nicole James, Heather Potter, and Ken Hampton for their unfailing help and patience in helping this manuscript get to print in time, to Dee Cole for helping with the proof reading, and Gaye Hodges for providing those welcome cups of tea and coffee, and to Michael Hodges for his patience and understanding when taking the pictures for this book. Many thanks to you all for your help.

Evelyn Curtis

Introduction

IT'S NEARLY always assumed if you write about cooking, you must be a first class cook, that you can whip up feather light soufflés at the drop of a wooden spoon, and your cakes and sponges pick up first prize at any local fete or show – if that definition sounds too good to be true, believe me, it is. My cooking is the kind you would find in most family kitchens, with good old fashioned puds, airy light sponges with crisp golden tops, rich brown casseroles, and succulent joints of meat heading the list, and I have to admit, the Aga and I have an ongoing love affair when we get together on a cold winter's afternoon for a baking session.

Now, add the word "people" to cooking, and my interest is heightened, cooking then takes second place, with people and writing becoming my main ingredients. It was this combination which gave me the idea to write a book about both, and eventually became the title 'My Kind of People – My Kind of Cooking'.

One of the things I enjoy most is walking round a Farmer's Market on a Saturday morning, seeing all the home produced products on display. Go to one of these markets in winter time and you will see beef in beer casseroles bubbling away on portable stoves, the farmer's wife or his assistant will offer you a bowl of the rich steaming liquid to sample, before you carry on walking round the market stalls on a cold winter's morning. Sausages splutter and sizzle in frying pans, almost bursting out of their skins, as they cook in the hot oil, and the farmer standing by his stall has maybe as many as 12 different varieties to offer you, some with exotic sounding names like Sundried Tomato and Oregano, and others with more traditional names like Port and Stilton, and Pork and Leek, displayed alongside the colourful Lemon and Pepper Herb Steaks, Garlic and Onion Spare Ribs, and Roulades of Pork with Sun Dried Tomatoes and Wild Mushrooms, which is the latest new product from Sue and Ian Whitehead's farm shop in Brundish, Suffolk.

So now our farmers have become cooks, experimenting with all kinds of herbs to promote and tempt us to buy their meat, doing most of the preparation work for us, thereby saving us a lot of time – no more marinating or stuffing of joints, we can just pop the meat into the oven straightaway or freeze it for a later date – definitely "my kind of cooking"!

And then we have a housewife, who, although she cooks most of the day in a local hotel, goes home and bakes superb wedding and birthday cakes, and attends evening classes so that she can learn how to ice them professionally. At my local bakery we are spoilt for choice; Anne Faiers the lady baker, and her sons, bake no less than 20 different varieties of loaves and rolls each day, as well as a variety of cakes and scones. Open the shop door and you will see baskets of "knotted", seeded and granary rolls piled in miniature pyramids alongside huffers and milky soft rolls, which Anne has just brought in from the bakehouse, the aroma of freshly baked bread and cakes tempting you before you even reach the counter.

These are just some of the "my kind of people" I have written about, they come from all walks of life, but all have one thing in common, they enjoy cooking and eating good home produced food, some making a living by selling their produce too. All have interesting stories to tell. In the farming industry the crisis in agriculture has prompted a lot of farmers to diversify into new ventures to keep their farms going, and I believe this is how farmers' markets first started. Others have opted out of the rat race, moving from the capital into the countryside, where they now run cosy little tearooms and restaurants. Homemade cakes, quiches and soups are prepared and cooked by husband and wife teams, or dedicated cooks and helpers from surrounding villages.

I've tried to make the first part of this book a colourful tapestry about people's lives, telling their stories as they told them to me, all are interwoven with a background of food and cooking, some have an air of surprise about them, some nostalgia. Who would have thought one of our local choir ladies flew in a Wellington Bomber on a test flight during the Second World War, or that the sprightly 93 year old I interviewed last March, became a Leading Aircraft Woman in the last war, but had her career cut short when she had to return home to nurse her sick mother, and one young man despaired of ever finding his soul mate, only to go on and marry one of the most attractive girls in the village, who just happens to be a fabulous cook too.

I've listened to their stories, and my computer and I have lived in their lives for the past 12 months, gaining me many new friends. My thanks go out to all of them for turning back *their pages*, and allowing me the privilege to *look inside*, for without them this book could not have been written. It may have started out as just *another cookbook*, but I hope when you read it, you'll agree it's one with a difference!

Evelyn Curtis

PART ONE

My Kind of People

 Dewi Owen

 Regis Crepy

 Sarah Boosé

 Felicity Pocock

 Eva King

 Elsie Hynard

 Margaret Morley

 Richard Evans

 Beth Raine

 Sally Bendall

 Nellie King

 Abi Kelly

 Robert Bendall

 Anne Faiers

 Pam Gray

 Ian Whitehead

 John Heeks

 Rosemary Wheeler

 Sue Whitehead

 Win Gage

My Kind of People

FELICITY POCOCK AND
   JOHN YOUDELL 11
   Parsnip and Lemon Soup 12
   Sausage and Celery Stuffing ... 12
   Westmorland Lamb Hot-Pot ... 12
   Cumberland Pie 13
   Three-Chocolate Sponge
      Puddings 13

ANNE FAIERS 14
   Pommes Dauphine 15
   Queen of Puddings 15
   Lager Loaf 16

SUE AND IAN WHITEHEAD 17
   Vegetable Soup 18
   Pork Medallions with
      Peppercorn Sauce 18
   Summer Pudding 19

BETH RAINE 20
   Beth's Roasted Red Peppers ... 21
   Steak Casserole 21
   Lemon Mousse 21

REGIS CREPY 22
   Asparagus Flan 23
   Bavarois a la Crème et aux
      Framboises 23

THÉRÈSA TOLLEMACHE &
   ABI KELLY 24
   Caribbean Chicken or Turkey ... 25
   Saucy Chocolate Pudding 26
   Hazelnut Coffee Cake 26

ELSIE HYNARD 27
   Cheesy Bread & Butter
      Pudding 28
   Apple Pudding 28
   Red Fruit Flan 29

EVA KING 30
   Smoked Salmon Terrine 31
   Lemon and Tarragon Chicken
      Parcel 32
   Hazelnut & Lemon Gateau 32
   Oat & Apricot Crumbles 33

JOHN HEEKS 34
   Devilled Bacon and Mushroom
      Cups 36
   Chicken with Lemon & Almond ... 36

Apricot Wholewheat Syrup
   Pudding 37

SARAH BOOSÉ 38
   Courgette Bake 39
   Texas Style Pumpkin Pie 39

ROSEMARY WHEELER 40
   Pork and Sage Parcels 42
   Pot Roast Brisket with Root
      Vegetables 42
   English Lamb with Asparagus ... 43

MARGARET MORLEY 44
   Rabbit Pie 45
   Apple Pie 45
   Date and Walnut Bread 46

WIN GAGE 47
   Chicken and Vegetable Soup ... 48
   Chicken and Herb Pasta 48
   Lemon Meringue Pie 49
   Caramel Slice 49

MEINIR AND DEWI OWEN 50
   Herby Penmaen Lamb 51
   Sweet Esgair Lamb 52
   Spicy Maethlon Lamb 52
   Apple Crumble 53

PAM GRAY 54
   Courgette & Cumin Soup 55
   Parsnip & Apple Soup 55
   Lemon Drizzle Cake 55
   Queen Mother Cake 56
   Lavender Cake 56

SALLY AND ROBERT BENDALL ... 57
   Baked Ham 58
   Rhubarb Crisp 58
   Chilled Lemon Flan 59

NELLIE SMITH 60
   Meat Balls in Tomato Sauce ... 62
   Apricot Tart 62
   Cherry and Preserved Ginger
      Cake 63

RICHARD EVANS 64
   Steak and Kidney Pudding 65
   Beef in Beer 65
   Any 'Old' Fruit Upside-Down
      Pudding 66

Felicity Pocock and John Youdell

A teashop, restaurant, and food hampers, an unusual combination, but one that works well for Felicity Pocock and John Youdell. This enterprising couple have now been running their business for the past 10 years, food hampers playing a large part, with orders coming in from both mail order and from sales in the shop.

Felicity Pocock owns and runs Lakeland Hampers with her partner John Youdell. John is the son of Harold Youdell, who was a well-known wine merchant in Kendal. John originally worked in his father's business, importing sherry and port in oak casks, which they bottled and labelled themselves. Naturally some of their customers were large companies, who gave Christmas gifts to their staff, so introducing hampers to their customers seemed like a good idea to John.

Operating initially from home, with a warehouse for storage, and with the intention of targeting local businesses, John was able to put his idea into practice. In the weeks leading up to Christmas 1989 Lakeland Hampers became so popular that John and Felicity took a temporary site in the shopping centre in Kendal. They were so successful they decided to go for a more permanent retail outlet and combine it with a teashop/restaurant, and so the Lakeland Hampers Tearoom was well and truly launched, and has been going strong ever since.

Hampers offer traditional food in their restaurant with lunchtime specials such as homemade Chicken and Leek and Cumberland pies. Puddings are the 'to die for' ones, with enticing names such as Chocolate Sponge Pudding, and Speech House Pudding, and there's a wonderful range of ice creams from English Lakes Ice Cream.

Teatime is well catered for, with scones, crumpets, cinnamon toast and a whole host of scrumptious cakes ready to comfort the weary shopper.

Felicity tells me everything is made by them to regional recipes, using local ingredients, or it's made in the county, for example, their lunchtime game pie and sausages come from Slacks of Orton, and the Ultimate Plum Pudding is made in Kendal – food with a truly Cumbrian flavour.

Their leaflets list the hampers you can buy and send to friends and relatives, or you can just treat yourself to one, all brimming with the very best of Cumbrian foods. The Windermere, which is the most expensive hamper, is priced at £135 and offers a treasure trove of goodies resting in an attractive buff willow hamper, but you could spend as little as £25 and still have excellent value for your money. All these goodies and luxuries have been carefully chosen and attractively packaged, showing the same care and attention which has gone into the Lakeland Hampers Tearoom.

Here are some of the enticingly named recipes that appear daily on the Lakeland Tea Room's menu.

PARSNIP AND LEMON SOUP

Serves 6

450g (1lb) parsnips, peeled and
 chopped
35g (1½oz) butter
1 litre (1¾ pints) vegetable stock
Zest and juice of half a lemon
Salt and pepper
2 medium onions, chopped
Pinch of mixed herbs
4 sprigs of lemon balm

Heat butter in a pan and sauté the chopped onions and herbs. Add peeled and chopped parsnips and fry gently for a few minutes. Add stock, salt, pepper, lemon zest and juice. Cook until parsnips are very soft. Liquidise and add milk or cream to taste, depending on how thick you like your soup. Decorate with lemon balm before serving.

SAUSAGE AND CELERY STUFFING

*This is a useful stuffing to stuff your turkey with at Christmas-time.
However, I found it also made very tasty burgers coated in breadcrumbs
and fried in hot oil, then sandwiched between baps or crusty rolls.*

450g (1lb) Cumberland sausage
 meat
4 sticks of celery, chopped and de-
 stringed
1 large onion finely chopped
1 egg
1 crust of bread crumbed
Salt and pepper
10g (½oz) butter

Sauté onion in butter. Add celery and cook for a few minutes. Combine all ingredients in a bowl and mix thoroughly. Stuff the neck of your Christmas turkey with this – Felicity says "I always make extra, as everyone loves it".

WESTMORLAND LAMB HOT-POT

1kg (2lb) diced lamb shoulder
1 black pudding (approx. 225g)
 (8oz)
3 medium carrots
½ medium swede
1½kg (3lb) potatoes, peeled and
 sliced
1 large onion
Salt, pepper and mixed herbs
1 lamb stock cube
10g (½oz) butter

Slice onion and sauté in butter with herbs. Brown lamb with onions and add stock cube, seasoning and water to cover meat. Simmer for 30 minutes, adding chopped carrot and swede for last 10 minutes, plus slightly more water if needed. In a casserole dish layer meat mixture with sliced potatoes, adding slices of black pudding with the meat. Finish with a layer of potatoes and add remaining liquid. Cook in preheated oven 200C, 400F, Gas Mark 6 until top is brown and meat is tender. Serve with pickled red cabbage.

CUMBERLAND PIE

700g (1½lb) Cumberland sausage
  meat
(Cumberland sausage meat is
  coarser in texture and usually
  has a higher percentage of
  meat)
1 large onion
tsp mixed herbs
1 crust of bread made into crumbs
1 egg
Salt and pepper
50g (2oz) butter
1¼kg (2½lb) potatoes

Chop the onion and mix in bowl
with sausage meat, herbs, breadcrumbs and egg until thoroughly
combined. Put into ovenproof
lasagne dish squashing out until
the bottom of the dish is covered.
Place in preheated oven 200C,
400F, Gas Mark 6 for 20 minutes.
Peel, chop and boil the potatoes
until soft. Mash potatoes and add
10g (½oz) of butter, salt, pepper
and milk or cream, for a really
creamy dish. Place on top of
cooked sausage meat, dot with
remaining butter and bake for
another 20 minutes, or until
browned on top.

THREE-CHOCOLATE SPONGE PUDDINGS

*(i.e. three chocolates in one pudding,
or individual puddings)*
Serves 4

50g (2oz) cocoa
110g (4oz) butter
225g (8oz) self-raising flour
110g (4oz) caster sugar
2 eggs
2 tbsp milk

For the sauce:
175g (6oz) chocolate (dark, white
  or milk)
3 tbsp golden syrup
3 tbsp milk
10g (½oz) butter

Melt chocolate and stir in other
sauce ingredients. Place tables-
poon of sauce in small pudding
basins (I use small plastic ones,
approximately 10cm (4") diameter).
   For the pudding: Rub dry
ingredients for puddings together
and then mix with eggs and milk.
Spoon mixture on top of sauce,
and cover each pudding with
greaseproof paper, tucked and held
in place with a rubber band. Steam
in pan with lid on in 2 inches of
water for 40 minutes. Serve with
custard which you have melted
chocolate into – i.e. chocolate
pudding, with chocolate sauce and
chocolate custard.

DELICIOUS!

Anne Faiers

With many village shops closing down around the countryside, in Lavenham we are fortunate in having a baker, grocer, greengrocer, butcher and a newsagent, as well as a Post Office, in fact it's a very self sufficient place to live.

Go into Sparling and Faiers bakery on any day, and you may spot a small, trim figure dart into the shop from the back with a tray of bread, and then quickly out again, it will probably be Anne Faiers, who moves as quick as lightening. Anne now runs the family bakery, which until a few years ago her brother, Leonard Sparling, ran with her. Situated in the Market Square and surrounded by picturesque buildings, many dating back to the fourteenth century, it draws a lot of customers from tourists to Lavenham.

Anne's grandfather, Harry Hector Sparling, was a baker in Southend. In the late 1800s, before he became a baker, her grandfather was a chef on a yacht, and she still has the Golden Sovereign, which the German Kaiser presented to him, and other members of the crew, when he was a guest on the yacht. She also remembers her father telling her, and her brother and sisters, many tales of when he was a young lad delivering bread to colourful customers like the showmen in Kursal Amusement Park, and the very long hours it took before they finished their rounds, sometimes not getting home until very late at night.

Anne's parents carried on the bakery tradition and started their own business in Colchester, where she was born. All the children had to help in the bakery when they came home from school, and one of the jobs they had to do was greasing the bread tins ready for the next day's baking, a job they hated! She also remembers delivering bread with her father in a horse-drawn cart.

The Sparling family moved to Lavenham in 1950, and Leonard Sparling worked with his father Harry, who taught him the bakery business. His father retired in 1969, and Len's brother-in-law, Les Faiers, joined the business with his wife, Anne. Les, a local man, had worked with the previous owner of the bakery, but had also farmed and been a builder. Les died some nine years ago, and the business continued to be run by the brother and sister team, with Len concentrating on the bread and Anne looking after the confectionery side of the business. Two other sisters used to help out in the bakery before leaving to get married, and both Len and Anne's sons also joined the business, carrying on the tradition of working and running a thriving family bakery.

Leonard Sparling has now moved away from Lavenham, Anne is still kept busy in the bakery, and lives on the premises. When she is not baking, gardening is her hobby, and seeing her garden for the first time this summer was testament to how much hard work, and love of plants, has gone into the making of this little piece of Eden.

Anne has given me some of her favourite recipes; the first recipe comes from the Provence of France. She often cooks this dish and says it makes a tasty supper, but is robust enough for a main meal.

POMMES DAUPHINE

Serves 6

1 clove garlic, peeled and crushed
  (optional)
2 tbsp butter
750g (1lb10oz) potatoes, peeled
  and thinly sliced
115g (4½oz) grated yellow cheese
6 tbsp butter cut into very small
  dice
Salt and pepper
225ml (8floz) half and half milk
  and cream (use a little more if
  needed)

Rub the bottom and sides of a heavy baking dish with the crushed clove of garlic. Grease the bottom and sides liberally with butter. Spread half of the potato slices in the bottom of the dish, sprinkle with half of the cheese, some salt and pepper, and dot with half the butter. Top with the remaining slices of potato, neatly arranged. Sprinkle with the remaining cheese, salt and pepper, and butter. Pour the cream down the inside of the dish around the potatoes. Cook in the top part of an oven pre-heated to 200C, 400F, Gas Mark 6 for 30–40 minutes, or until the potatoes are tender and the top is nicely browned. Serve immediately.

QUEEN OF PUDDINGS

Serves 4

300ml (½pt) milk
Zest of 1 small lemon
10g (½oz) butter
25g (1oz) caster sugar
50g (2oz) fresh white breadcrumbs
2 eggs
2–3 tbsp strawberry or raspberry
  jam, slightly warmed
110g (4oz) caster sugar for the
  meringue

Bring milk to boil in saucepan and add lemon rind. Strain into a bowl, add the butter, sugar and bread-crumbs, stirring well so that sugar is dissolved. Leave for about 20 minutes to allow breadcrumbs to swell, and when cool add egg yolks and mix thoroughly, and turn into a lightly buttered 850ml (1½ pint pie dish). Bake in pre-heated oven 180C, 350F, Gas Mark 4 for about 25–30 minutes, or until set. Remove, cool slightly and spread warmed jam over the top. Whip egg whites until firm, then fold in sugar, keeping back 1 tsp. Pile meringue on top of pudding and dust over with the remaining tsp of caster sugar. Bake for a further 12–15 minutes reducing heat to 170C, 325F, Gas Mark 3, until the meringue is set and golden brown.

LAGER LOAF

This loaf smells delicious when cooking, and is even more delicious sliced and buttered for tea. It will keep well, and doesn't go dry quickly – freezes well too.

75g (3oz) butter
1 tbsp golden syrup or treacle
75g (3oz) soft brown sugar
2 eggs
275g (10oz) self-raising flour
¼ tsp bicarbonate of soda
½ tsp cream of tartar
Pinch of salt
150ml (¼ pint) lager
2 bananas, peeled and mashed
110g (4oz) dates, chopped
50g (2oz) walnuts, chopped

Well grease a 900g (2lb) loaf tin or two 450g (1lb) loaf tins. Gently heat the butter, syrup and sugar in a saucepan until melted. Remove from heat and whisk the eggs into the mixture. Sift flour, bicarbonate of soda, cream of tartar and salt into a bowl. With a wooden spoon briskly mix in the syrup mixture and add the lager. Mix to a smooth batter, and then quickly add the mashed bananas, chopped dates and walnuts. Pour the mixture into the prepared loaf tin (or tins). Bake in the centre of a preheated oven 180C, 350F, Gas Mark 4, for 1½ hours. Turn out onto a cake rack and cool. Serve sliced and buttered.

Sue and Ian Whitehead

Sue and Ian Whitehead have been running Lane Farm Country Foods since 1987 and work from sun up to sun down in the running of their business.

Their dream to buy their own farm came about in 1980 when they both went travelling around in New Zealand, studying the various farming techniques there.

Although Sue comes from a farming family (her grandmother, Peggy Risk, was one of the first lady students at Chadacre in the 1930s, and it is from her recipe book the Suffolk Farmhouse sausage comes from), Ian had only recently come into agriculture also by way of being a Chadacre student.

Eventually they found and managed to purchase Lane Farm, two days before Rebecca their daughter was born. The purchase was finalised on 10 October 1987, the time of the terrible gales that racked havoc throughout the country. Sue and Ian lost half their farm buildings, which blew away in these terrible gales, and had to set to and rebuild most of them.

They then spent the next 9–10 years building up a High Health Status Pig herd and selling Multiplication Breeding Stock to other farms, even exporting some to Europe.

After just coming out of a bad recession 5 years ago, they decided to invest in their own EU approved plant and process their own pigs for local shops and restaurants. This came about after a day trip together to North Norfolk where they saw lots of pigs being bred in outdoor units. Taking this plunge has paid off and Sue was able to give up her job as a Freelance Farm Secretary enabling her to work full-time in the butchery, with Ian spending more time on the marketing and general running of the business.

They are continually seeking new ideas, and trying out new recipes for their different sausages. Sue says, "as with everything they have done at Lane Farm, from breeding High Health pigs, to producing high meat content sausages, they aim to do everything just that little bit better than their counterparts", and back bacon is cured the old-fashioned way, leaving it to air dry before slicing.

Sue and Ian are regulars at Farmers' Markets in and around the country, even travelling as far as Islington in London, selling their produce. I've now been a customer for the past two years, buying their own dry cured bacon, sausages and joints of pork all produced from their prime cuts of meat. The aroma of their bacon cooking in my kitchen brings back memories to me of how bacon used to taste and smell, when a joint of pork came out of the oven succulent and juicy, with the crackling all crisp and golden ready for carving.

With the recession farming is going through today, Sue and Ian hope that with their combined hard work and effort, together with a real desire to produce the best products, will hopefully help them through the recession farming is in today.

Although with not much time to spare, Sue enjoys cooking for her family, and has contributed three of her most used recipes for my book. Naturally pork figures high on her cooking list. I liked the sound of pork medallions cooked in butter and served with a green peppercorn sauce, which she often cooks, and her grandmother's vegetable soup, and although Sue rarely cooks desserts, summer pudding is made at least 2 or 3 times a year during the summer months when the fresh juicy fruit arrives.

VEGETABLE SOUP

Serves 6

75g (3oz) butter
1 leek sliced
1 large onion, peeled and chopped
2 sticks of celery, washed and
  chopped
1 large carrot, scraped and sliced
2 large potatoes, peeled and cut
  into quarters
1 clove garlic
1 tbsp parsley
1 dsp tomato puree (or three whole tomatoes)
1 litre (1¾ pints) chicken stock

Melt butter in large pan and add vegetables, cooking until just golden brown. Add crushed garlic and stock and simmer for about 1½ hours. Add salt and pepper to taste, and then liquidize. Sprinkle with chopped parsley when serving.

PORK MEDALLIONS WITH PEPPERCORN SAUCE

Serves 4

450g (1lb) fillet of pork, cut into 4
  medallions
1 egg, beaten
75g (3oz) breadcrumbs
Knob of butter for frying

Flatten each medallion with the heal of the hand and coat in breadcrumbs and egg. Melt butter in frying pan and fry medallions. When cooked set aside on serving plate and keep warm.

For the sauce:
3 tbsps green peppercorns
150ml (¼ pint) double cream
50ml (2floz) dry white wine
10g (½oz) butter

To make the sauce: Melt butter in pan. Add green peppercorns and wine, heat through, then add the cream and stir briskly until sauce reduces a little and thickens, making sure you do not boil it, otherwise the cream will curdle. Pour over medallions and serve with new potatoes and a green vegetable.
Delicious.

SUMMER PUDDING

If you miss out on the fresh fruit season, then mixed frozen fruits will do just as well.

10–12 slices of white day old bread, with crust cut off
110g (4oz) raspberries
110g (4oz) strawberries
110g (4oz) blackcurrants
50g (2oz) redcurrants
50g (2oz) blackberries
75g (3oz) caster sugar

Clean and pick over fruit. Place fruit in large saucepan with sugar and 2 tbsps water. Bring to a gentle simmer over a very low heat, and cook for 3–4 minutes until juices begin to run. Remove from heat and set aside. Cut crusts from bread slices and cut a round of bread from one slice to fit the base of a 1.5 litre (2½ pint) pudding basin. Cut remaining slices in half lengthwise. Arrange bread slices around the side of basin, overlapping them at the bottom so that they fit neatly together. Spoon the fruit into the lined basin and set aside about 100ml (3½floz) of fruit juice and spoon the remainder into the fruit filled basin. Cover with remaining bread slices, trimming to fit where necessary. Cover the pudding with a saucer that fits inside the top of the pudding basin and set a weight on the saucer 700g (1½lb) to 1kg (2¼lb). Chill in fridge overnight. When ready to serve, turn out and coat with remaining juice. Cut out in required portions and serve with clotted cream or ice cream.

Beth Raine

Chances are if you go into the Swan Hotel in Lavenham, you will see an attractive young blonde bustling through the hotel's entrance hall, it will be Beth Raine, the hotel's General Manager. Beth is no stranger to the Swan Hotel, and had previously worked there in 1993, staying for three years.

As you can imagine, working in a busy hotel does not leave much time for giving interviews, but I have got to know Beth well over the past year, and have found her lively and interesting to talk to. From the small "chats" we have managed to have from time to time, I discovered that Beth's interest in cooking started at a very young age, and in Beth's own words...............

"I was born in 1967 in the small agricultural village of Brindle in the heart of Lancashire. My mother was always a keen cook, and at an early age I well remember helping her prepare for dinner parties and family gatherings, and I was the one usually left with the washing-up afterwards, but that didn't put me off cooking!

"In fact cooking quickly became one of my chief interests, and this was encouraged by my grandmother, who each year would make sure I submitted entries for the local village show. At school I always enjoyed Domestic Science lessons and achieved an O Level in Domestic Science and an A Level in Food and Nutrition.

"I became interested in working in the catering industry when I was 16 years old, and started a part-time job as a waitress in a local hotel, but I was keen to go to University, so after completing my A Levels, I started a BSc (Hons) in Hotel and Institutional Management at Cardiff University. I then joined Forte's Graduate Management Programme on completion of my degree, and worked across all their brands in Harrogate, Blackpool, Northampton and Milton Keynes, which gave me good grounding and experience in the catering and hotel trade.

"As I gained in knowledge and experience in hotel management and catering, I found that the smaller more individual properties appealed to me most, so in 1992 I joined the Heritage brand, and I moved to Suffolk in 1993 and to The Swan as their Catering Manager. I was here for over three years, and when I left I was their Deputy General Manager. It was then I moved on to The Crown of '4 Weddings and a Funeral' fame in Amersham, and stayed there for two years. At about this time I moved to Forte's Head Office in London to work on a customer service programme, and in 1999 I returned to The Swan as General Manager to oversee the closing down and full refurbishment of this lovely hotel, which is the oldest inn in Lavenham, and is a late 14th century building.

"Although I lead a busy working life, I still find time to travel, which is one of my main interests, and this year I have been to South Africa, Dubai and Portugal. I also love to cook and entertain at home, but leading a busy working life doesn't leave much spare time, so I find making casseroles in batches and then freezing them helps a lot, and there is always something in reserve for weekends or when friends drop in for a meal. These are three of my 'easy recipes'; the roasted red peppers are a meal in themselves, especially in the summer with a crisp green salad – ideal too if you're counting calories!"

BETH'S ROASTED RED PEPPERS

Serves 4

4 large red peppers
8 cherry plum tomatoes
8 garlic cloves
8 tbsp Italian extra virgin olive oil
3 fillets of anchovy (optional)
Freshly ground black pepper

Cut the peppers around the stalks and remove the seeds. Halve the peppers lengthways and lay in a lightly oiled roasting tray. Place inside each pepper 1 cherry plum tomato and 1 garlic clove. Chop the anchovy fillets and sprinkle onto each half pepper then add the olive oil. Season with ground black pepper. Place in preheated oven 180C, 350F, Gas Mark 4 on a tray on a high shelf in the oven and roast the peppers for about 1 hour. Place the 8 half peppers onto a serving dish with all the juices poured over. Garnish each half pepper with a sprig of basil. Serve with thick slices of ciabatta bread.

STEAK CASSEROLE

'a recipe for busy career women and busy housewives'!
Serves 4

700g (1½lb) chuck steak
1 large onion
Flour seasoned with salt and
    pepper
1 med. tin condensed tomato soup
2 tbsp mushroom ketchup
2 tbsp red wine (optional) or stock
3 rashers of bacon

Cut steak into small pieces and rub in seasoned flour, dice bacon and onion, then fry bacon and onion, then steak 5–8 minutes. Put all in a casserole, add soup, ketchup, wine or stock and seasoning, cover with a lid and cook in a very slow oven 140C, 275F, Gas Mark 1 for 3½ hours. A little more or less will not matter. The meat emerges beautifully tender and the gravy rich and brown. If you wish to make the dish very special, add a tin of ratatouille about ½ hour before serving.

LEMON MOUSSE

Serves 4

3 leaves of gelatine or 1 sachet of
    gelatine powder
75ml (3floz) water
3 egg yolks
225g (8oz) caster sugar
2 lemons
300ml (½ pint) cream

Soak gelatine in the water and heat if necessary to ensure that the gelatine is thoroughly dissolved. Take the zest from the lemons and squeeze out all the juice. Place over heat and bring to the boil. Remove from the heat and add to the dissolved gelatine. Separate eggs. Place the yolks with the sugar in a bowl and whisk over a pan of hot water until light in colour. Cool the lemon juice mixture and add it to the eggs and sugar. Place this mixture in the fridge until it reaches setting point. Remove and add the semi whipped cream. Pour into ramekins or onto a sponge base.

Regis Crepy

I first met Regis Crepy in December, 1986. It was a bitterly cold Boxing Day, my husband and I, and our daughter, had driven over from the East Coast to have lunch at The Swan Hotel in Lavenham. Unfortunately we hadn't booked, and they were full. At that time Lavenham wasn't our "stamping ground", but we thought we would find a decent pub and at least have a drink.

Walking around the market square we came across one of Lavenham's beautiful 14th century houses, and saw that it was a restaurant called The Great House. We later learnt that it used to be the home of poet Stephen Spender. Once inside we saw a huge fireplace with a blazing log fire, carved oak beams, tables were set in the dining room with snowy white cloths, with gleaming cutlery and sparkling wine glasses, and all the tables were full. Then Regis, and his wife Martine appeared, our coats were whisked away and we were soon seated beside a roaring fire with our drinks, and assured that a table would be laid for us in no time, in fact the welcome couldn't have been warmer.

It is so long ago now, I can't remember what we had to eat, but I do know it was a memorable meal, and we have returned again and again to eat there, and the Great House has been one of our favourite restaurants to celebrate family birthdays and special occasions. We now know Regis not only as chef-restaurateur of The Great House, but can count both him and Martine as our very good friends.

Regis was brought up in Lille, in northern France, and studied at the University of Lausanne, Switzerland, where he gained his Master's degree, and met Martine there, also a student, who was to become his wife. By the time they both arrived in England Regis had a varied experience of running a number of successful hotels, and Martine was expecting their first child, Emily. They spent a few months in London and Hertfordshire, before moving to Suffolk and taking over the management of The Great House, and eventually the ownership in 1992.

He has been so successful in Lavenham that he now owns and runs the former Italian restaurant called "Il Punto" in Ipswich. It is situated on a Dutch gunboat moored at the docks, and has since been converted into a French Brasserie. He has also taken over "Maison Bleue" in the heart of historic Bury St. Edmunds. This was formerly known as Mortimer's, and Regis has wisely continued the tradition of it being primarily known as a fish restaurant. He now wants to expand into Cambridge, and I am sure that he will, as there is simply no stopping this genial and enterprising Frenchman's quest to explore and conquer new avenues, his enthusiasm for good food and cooking is endless.

Martine plays a large part in helping to run this family business, and shoulders much of the responsibility for the Lavenham restaurant, whilst Regis maintains an overall view of the business, making it very much a team job. Since I first met Martine and Regis their family has grown, Emily is now 16 and has a ten-year old brother, Alexander, and the family have well and truly made Lavenham their home for the past 15 years, as Regis says, "we have a quality of life here, and are very happy in Lavenham, it is a beautiful village with lots of interesting buildings and people, and we have made many friends, here".

Getting recipes from Regis is no mean feat, they usually start with 20 eggs etc., etc., but I have managed to prise two from him for my book, all typically French and, naturally, all using the very best of ingredients!

ASPARAGUS FLAN

Take a bunch of asparagus and cook it for about 8 to 10 minutes in very salted boiling water. Do not cover.

For each 100g of asparagus cooked, set aside 100g of crème and 1 egg.

Put the asparagus in a food mixer and puree them.

Put the asparagus puree onto a frying pan and cook under slow heat to dry the puree.

Mix asparagus, cream and eggs in a bowl.

Salt and pepper the mixture.

Transfer the mixture into individual ramekins and cook in a Bain Marie for 30 minutes at 180C, 350F, Gas Mark 4.

Serve with a hollandaise sauce and a glass of dry white wine.

BAVAROIS a la CRÈME et aux FRAMBOISES

(this is a delicious creamy raspberry dessert)

For the vanilla crème:
1 litre milk
10 egg yolks
250g (9oz) sugar
1 vanilla pod
2 decilitres de crème

Heat the milk with the vanilla pod.

Beat the egg yolks and sugar together until fluffy.

Pour the boiling milk onto the egg mixture and reduce the heat (87C).

Add the cream and take the vanilla pod out.

For the Bavarois:
8 decilitres* vanilla cream
6 leaves of gelatine, put in water for 5 mins. to soften
4 decilitres* double cream
12 ramekins
Sufficient raspberries

Take the vanilla cream while hot and add leaves of gelatine.

Beat the double cream to a soft peak, and add to the vanilla cream mixture slowly when it starts to set.

Take 12 ramekins and put at the bottom 10 raspberries in each.

Fill the ramekins with the cream mixture and leave to set in fridge for one hour.

Bon appetit!

* A decilitre is 1/10th of a litre.

The Volga Linen Story
as told to me by
Thérèsa Tollemache & Abi Kelly

I suppose you could say that I discovered Abi Kelly under a bolt of linen, but that would be exaggerating. However, it is true to say she was surrounded by shelves piled high with linen, in the office base of the Volga Linen Company, when I first met her.

Abi looks after Thérèsa Tollemache, the founder of this company, who set up her office and warehouse on an industrial estate in Leiston, Suffolk. Her forbearers are Russian, and it was on a pilgrimage to the land of her forbearers that she became interested in linen. This started from buying linen tea towels to take home from Russia to give to friends, which prompted them to ask why she didn't start importing linen. Producing linen is one of the oldest industries in Russia, and when travelling around and checking out factories over there she discovered wonderful linen being produced in ancient medieval cities and villages.

Thérèsa now imports linen to England, and in the Suffolk warehouse, beautiful damask tablecloths, linen dressing gowns, pillow cases, sheets and duvet covers are all carefully folded and stacked in creamy piles, some in delicate shades of blue, ready for despatch to her customers in England and abroad.

A lot of people, have the wrong perception in thinking linen as being stiff, cold and formal, but Thérèsa says "It's not so, this linen isn't at all like that, it's soft and comforting, it doesn't matter if you crumple it, and you shouldn't feel you have to iron out every wrinkle. People even say to me 'is it made from cotton', and I tell them, 'it comes from flax, a blue flower on a long stem containing the linen fibre. Russia and the Baltic States grow at least 80 percent of the world's flax, and you can see fields like blue oceans, but at the end of the summer it goes dry and golden'."

Her output has now quadrupled from her initial outlay to buy, manufacture, and import stocks of Russian linen, and she now sells by mail order, and specialises in London shops in Notting Hill and Kensington.

Abi is the one who will answer the telephone and deal with your order in a quick and efficient manner. If you call to pick up your linen, as I did, then it will be handed to you in a shiny cream tote bag, all beautifully folded and tied up in burgundy ribbon. It is obvious that Thérèsa depends on Abi for the smooth running of her Suffolk operation, and can go away on her buying trips to Russia, knowing full well she has left her company in good hands.

After I had met Thérèsa I got talking to Abi, and I asked her if she ever felt isolated or lonely working on her own in the middle of an industrial estate, with micro light manufacturers next door for neighbours, but this tiny elfish young woman quickly assured me she wasn't. It was obvious she shared Thérèsa's passion for linen, but I wondered what had led her to The Volga Linen Company, and this is what Abi told me.

"I was born in Hertfordshire and moved to Suffolk with my parents when I was 15. I went to Suffolk College and studied catering, not sure then what I really wanted to do with my life. After college I got a job as a chef in The Crown at Westleton, which is near Dunwich, and I spent 4½ happy years there, but the hours were long and I found it encroached on my social life. So I decided to go back to college again, and I studied business administration and typing. This training came in very useful and I was able to take up a post in Leiston Post Office. During my five years working at the Post Office I progressed from working on the counter to becoming joint manager. It was whilst working at the Post Office that Thérèsa Tollemache approached me. She said she needed someone to help her with the running of the Volga Linen Company, and wondered if I would be interested. It was quite a challenge, but something different, so I handed in my notice and left the Post Office, and I haven't regretted leaving for one moment. Thérèsa is away a lot, and I more or less have a free hand in running the office, so there is plenty to keep me occupied and busy, and surrounded by all this lovely linen what could be better!

"I recently got married to Andrew Hassett, and we live in a 1930's house in Aldeburgh. I used to live in Woodbridge and was involved in voluntary work with the Woodbridge Gateway Club for the handicapped. We take groups away for holidays, usually at a Holiday Camp. We try to go away when it's out of season, and other handicapped groups are there, so we can organise games and all sorts of things to keep them occupied and happy. I don't think I would like to cook on a large catering scale again, but I do like cooking at home and experimenting with different ingredients, and I'll let you have some of my recipes". *And Abi was as good as her word!*.........

CARIBBEAN CHICKEN OR TURKEY

Serves 2

2 chicken or turkey breasts
2 tsp oil
1 small onion, peeled and chopped
1 med. green pepper, seeded and
   chopped
2 tsp cornflour
110g (4oz) pineapple
2 tbsp pineapple juice
2 tbsp tomato sauce
2 tsp curry powder
300ml (½ pint) chicken stock
Salt and pepper to taste
1 medium banana

Fry meat, transfer to casserole dish. Fry onion and pepper, transfer to casserole dish. Blend cornflour with pineapple juice, tomato sauce, curry powder, stock and seasoning. Pour over meat and add pineapple. Cook for 1 hour in preheated oven 180C, 350F, Gas Mark 4. Five minutes before the end of cooking, add the sliced banana. Serve with green salad and rice.

SAUCY CHOCOLATE PUDDING

During cooking, the water sinks through the pudding mixture making a thick chocolate sauce underneath.

Serves 4–5

110g (4oz) self-raising flour
110g (4oz) soft margarine
110g (4oz) Barbados sugar
30ml (2 tbsp) cocoa
2 eggs

Sauce:
45ml (3 tbsp) Barbados sugar
45ml (3 tbsp) cocoa
375ml (¾ pint) boiling water

Topping:
Demerara sugar

Place all pudding ingredients in a bowl and beat together until smooth and glossy. Transfer the mixture into a greased 1½ litre (2-pint) ovenproof dish and level the top with the back of a spoon.

Sauce:
Blend the sugar and cocoa with fingertips. Sprinkle over the pudding mixture and gently pour on the boiling water in a circular movement. Place dish on a baking sheet in preheated oven 180C, 350F, Gas Mark 4 for 35–40 mins. Sprinkle with demerara sugar and serve immediately.

HAZELNUT COFFEE CAKE

110g (4oz) butter or margarine
175g (6oz) soft brown sugar
2 eggs
6 tbsp milk
1 tbsp coffee essence
75g (3oz) hazelnuts
75g (3oz) raisins
225g (8oz) self-raising flour
1 tsp baking powder

Icing and decoration:
75g (3oz) butter or margarine
225g (8oz) icing sugar
1 tbsp coffee essence or 1 tbsp
  coffee dissolved in boiling water

Place all the ingredients in a bowl and beat with a wooden spoon until well mixed. Place in two greased 20cm (8 inch) sandwich tins. Bake in a moderate oven (160C, 325F, Gas Mark 3) for 30–40 minutes.

Turn out and cool on a wire tray. Prepare icing by mixing all ingredients together. Sandwich cakes together with a little of the icing, spread the remainder over the top of the cake. Pipe a border around the edge and decorate with whole toasted hazelnuts.

Variation: To make walnut coffee cake, substitute walnuts for hazelnuts.

Elsie Hynard

I first spotted Elsie Hynard singing lustily in the Lavenham Church Choir, a tall upright, kind, energetic woman, smartly turned out, and the sort not afraid to speak her mind. Someone suggested to me that Elsie would have an interesting story to tell, and that I should approach her and put her in my book. Well I did, and what an interesting tale she had to tell, there is definitely more to Elsie than meets the eye, and I wondered how her life would have been shaped had she been able to carry on serving in the forces after the war ended, instead of returning to Lavenham.

Elsie is a great stalwart in the Royal British Legion, having joined in 1946 she has been their secretary for 45 years, and is a member of the County Committee and acts as their Press Secretary, she also belongs to the over 60s, and is involved with other committees and organisations in the village, but let Elsie tell you her own story ......

"I was born in a cottage on Lavenham Hall Farm, Lavenham many years ago. My father was the Head Horseman, who loved his many Suffolk Punches, and he was never happier than when taking them to shows.

"My childhood days were very happy ones, and my friends and I spent many carefree days playing in the harvest fields around the farm buildings, except when the stallion visited, then we were banned.

"Schooldays were enjoyed very much, we had wonderful teachers, whom I remember with admiration and affection. We respected their discipline and patience, and looking back I realise how fortunate we were to have such dedicated teachers.

"The war came along in 1939 and, at the beginning of the war, I was employed in a factory in Barn Street, making kitbags and TNT bags for the war effort. This was a tedious job, and both my friend and I were getting very bored with this work, so we decided to volunteer for the WAAFs. We went for our medicals at Ipswich, and we passed A1, but this fact has an unexpected sequel, as you will see.

"The day came when we left home for the first time. We travelled from Lavenham Railway Station to London, and then on to Gloucester to be kitted out. From there, off we went to Morecambe to do our 'square bashing', we also had inoculations and x-rays etc. It was then that my friend was diagnosed as having T.B., so much to both our dismay her service was terminated.

"However, I was all right, and I eventually arrived in Scotland in the wilds of Angus, where I spent my first service days. When my training was over I spent the rest of my time working on aircraft, the first one was a Wellington bomber, which was used for training aircrew, and this was the first aircraft I flew in. When we worked on the 'planes we were allowed to fly on the test flight after servicing, and to me, it was all so thrilling and exciting, an experience never to be forgotten.

"Several airfields and 'planes later, and in spite of the war, I found that I was really enjoying my service life. Meeting people from all walks of life, the comradeship, and making wonderful friends is something I will never forget.

"When the war came to an end I was demobbed, and although I would have liked to have 'signed on' again, I had to return home to Lavenham to look after my mother who was not in the best of health. Living in Lavenham again seemed very dull, and it took ages for me to settle down, and although

I had had several boyfriends while I was away, I finally settled down and married a local lad. We had 49 happy years together, and although times were hard in those days, we came through them, and it made us appreciate all the simple things of life. We have come a long way since those days, it's called progress, but has it made folk happier – I wonder!"

Elsie's husband recently died, and although she now cooks for one, she gave me these three favourite recipes, telling me that *she still enjoys her 'apple pudding'*!

CHEESY BREAD & BUTTER PUDDING

This dish makes a tasty lunch or supper meal served with a crisp green salad.
Serves 4

4 large slices of buttered bread
110g–175g (4–6oz) grated cheese
Salt, pepper and mustard
1 tsp Worcestershire sauce
2 eggs
425ml (¾ pint) milk

Cut crusts from bread, cut each slice into six squares. Fill a greased 850ml (1½ pint) pie dish with alternate layers of bread and cheese. Season to taste and add Worcestershire sauce. Beat eggs and milk and strain over cheese. Sprinkle top with cheese and bake in the centre of a moderate oven for 45–50 minutes (preheated oven 170C–180C, 325–350F, Gas Mark 3–4.) Garnish with tomatoes and parsley.

APPLE PUDDING

Serves 3–4

225g (8oz) self-raising flour
110g (4oz) shredded suet
110g (4oz) caster sugar
450g (1lb) cooking apples
4 cloves
Water

Prepare suet pastry and turn onto floured board. Cut off about 1/3rd of pastry and line a pudding basin with the larger portion. Pare, core and slice apples, put half the apples in the basin and add sugar and cloves, then add the remainder of the apples and a little water. Roll out the smaller pastry portion and form into a round to fit top of basin, place on top of basin and press down the edges.

Cover with greased paper and foil, tie around with string and steam for 2 hours. Serve with custard.

RED FRUIT FLAN

Serves 4

110g (4oz) plain white or
  wholemeal flour
Pinch of salt
50g (2oz) butter or margarine
50g (2oz) caster sugar
2 egg yolks

Filling:
225g (8oz) low fat soft cheese with
  cherry
225g (8oz) fresh raspberries
225g (8oz) redcurrant jelly
225g (8oz) fresh strawberries,
  sliced

Sift flour and salt into a pastry bowl, make a well in the centre and add the butter, sugar and eggs together, and with the fingertips, gradually work in the flour until smooth. Wrap in a polythene bag and refrigerate for 1 hour before rolling out. Roll the pastry out to line a 20.5cm (8 inch) flan ring, prick the base and bake blind in preheated oven 190C, 375F, Gas Mark 5 for 12–15 minutes, then allow to cool. Spread the soft cheese onto the base, cover with the raspberries and strawberries. Simmer the redcurrant jelly until thick, and brush carefully over the fruit. Chill until ready to serve.

Eva King

Each year, on a Sunday, and usually in June, a number of people in Lavenham open their gardens to the public, and all the proceeds go to a worthy charity. Eva King has been opening her garden for many years, and goes even further by providing teas – the length of the queue of people standing outside her medieval cottage is proof of the popularity of these teas. Tables and chairs are set around Eva's lovely garden, and trays are laid with individual pots of tea and delicious home baked cakes. And, as Eva says, "Open Gardens Day is an opportunity for me to enjoy baking cakes without having to eat them."

Eva is an attractive grandmother, with merry, grey blue eyes twinkling in a face with a smooth unlined skin, framed with a halo of fair curly hair. When I recently called to see her, she proudly showed me her new kitchen, with its up-to-date pine cupboards and smooth workable work tops. It's obvious that Eva is happiest when baking in her kitchen for family and friends, and that she knew exactly what sort-of-kitchen she wanted when it was all being planned.

As it was a beautiful sunny day, one of those rare days when we look up to a brilliant blue sky and know that summer has finally arrived, and all the worries of the world disappear into the glorious sunshine, we went for a walk around her garden. Eva was quick to let me know that her husband Terry must take all the credit for the planning and planting, and it was obvious to see that over the years a lot of hard work had gone into the making of this lovely cottage garden. Shrubs are now tree high, in different shades of greens and yellows, making a soft backcloth for the roses, which were just coming into full bloom, and narrow winding paths encircled the trim green lawn. At the bottom of the garden tall trees and bushes look down onto Terry's organic vegetable patch, where potatoes, onions, carrots and cabbages are grown, and where, I suspect, small grandchildren play hide and seek, and make believe games.

As we sat in the garden talking, I looked at the cottages surrounding us, each radiating their own special history, with their tiny windows and sloping roofs, and Lavenham's lovely historical church peeping at us over the rooftops in the distance, I could quite easily have slipped back into a past century! But my reverie was suddenly broken by Eva's soft Suffolk tones telling me her story.........

"I was born in Lavenham and still live in the same house, No. 7 Bolton Street, where my parents and grandparents also lived. This house used to be an old wool store which was converted into cottages, and Bolton Street takes its name from Bolton's House, which belonged to John Bolton. Over the years the house has been enlarged and modernised by my husband, without changing it's medieval character.

"My mother died when I was nearly two years' old, and I went to live with an aunt, who brought me up. As I grew older I went back to live with my father and looked after him until he died. When I left school I trained as a hairdresser and worked in Long Melford, travelling to and fro by 'bus, in fact walking to the 'bus stop one morning was how I met my husband, Terry King. Terry, is one of the brothers of a thriving family building business in Lavenham. We have two children, Tracey, who trained as a nurse, and is now a Sister at the West Suffolk Hospital, and Richard, who now owns and runs a

Waste Skip Hire business. We have three grandchildren, Benjamin 7, Rebecca 3, and a fairly new arrival Jordan-Marie, who is just 8 months' old.

"About seventeen years ago, when my children were growing up, I started working in the bar at the Angel Hotel in Lavenham. I enjoyed this work and was able to meet many visitors to the village, as well as local friends and family coming into the bar for a drink or a meal. Over the years I progressed to working with the preparation of food, which I enjoy, and I then took over the making of desserts for the dining room, and learnt many other jobs both in the kitchen and hotel.

"I am still working at the Angel, chiefly making desserts, and cooking breakfasts when extra staff are needed during holiday times, in fact I can now turn my hand to most jobs in and around the kitchen and hotel. At home I like to indulge my hobby by making and decorating celebration cakes for friends and family, and at Christmas time I especially enjoy baking and icing mini Christmas cakes for the Hospice Xmas Sale and other bazaars.

"When my family and their children visit, or we have a big 'get together', it gives me a chance to try out some of my new ideas and recipes on them, and these are some family favourites, which are asked for again and again."

SMOKED SALMON TERRINE

Serves 4

350g (12oz) smoked salmon
½ tsp powdered gelatine
225g (8oz) fresh salmon
1 small onion, chopped
75ml (3floz) dry white wine
1 bay leaf
35g (1½oz) melted butter
75ml (3floz) double cream
1 tbsp chopped dill
Black pepper and salt

Line a 450g (1lb) loaf tin with ¾ of the smoked salmon slices, trimming and overlapping so that they fit neatly. Reserve rest of trimming for later. Sprinkle gelatine over approximately 2 tbsp of water, and set aside until spongy. Place the salmon in a small pan with the chopped onion, white wine and bay leaf. Cover and poach over a gentle heat for about 7–8 minutes or until just cooked. Leave to cool. Meanwhile dissolve gelatine over a pan of hot water and set aside. Remove the bay leaf and reserve the cooking juice and onion. Skin, bone and flake the salmon and place in a food processor with the smoked salmon, trimmings, cooking juices, gelatine, onion, butter, cream and dill, and process until smooth. Season to taste and pour into the prepared loaf tin. Chill for 2–3 hours until set. Use a knife to loosen terrine and turn onto a serving dish. Garnish with mixed salad leaves. Serve with crusty bread or toast.

LEMON AND TARRAGON CHICKEN PARCEL

Serves 4

1 onion, sliced
2 tbsp oil
450g (1lb) boned and skinned
   chicken breast, cut into 5cm
   (2 inch) pieces
25g (1oz) plain flour
200ml (7floz) milk
Grated zest and rind ½ lemon and
   2 tbsp juice
1 tbsp chopped fresh tarragon
Salt and pepper
450g (1lb) puff pastry (bought or
   home-made)
1 beaten egg

Fry onion in oil for about 5 mins.
Add chicken and cook for 5 mins to
brown slightly. Add flour and cook,
stirring for 1 minute, gradually stir
in milk, and cook stirring for 3
minutes.

Add lemon zest, juice, tarragon,
and seasoning. Simmer for 2
minutes and leave to cool for 15
minutes. Pre-heat oven to 220C,
425F, Gas Mark 7. Roll out puff
pastry to a 14 inch square and
place on baking sheet. Brush edges
with beaten egg and spoon filling
into the middle. Lift up corners,
pinch edges together and press
edges to seal. Brush with beaten
egg and bake for 25 minutes until
golden.

HAZELNUT & LEMON GATEAU

Serves 8–10

Cake:
4 eggs separated
110g (4oz) caster sugar
110g (4oz) ground hazelnuts
Grated rind of ½ lemon

Filling:
300ml (½ pint) double cream
2 tsp lemon juice
2 tbsp icing sugar
½ lemon sliced
11 whole hazelnuts

Pre-heat oven to 180C, 350F, Gas
Mark 4. Grease and flour 2 x
20.5cm (8 inch) spring clip, or loose
bottom tins. Put the egg yolks and
sugar in a bowl and whisk until
pale and thick. Mix in the ground
hazelnuts and lemon rind. Put the
whites into a clean grease free
bowl and whisk until it is standing
in stiff peaks. Fold the egg whites
into the hazelnut mixture. Divide
mixture equally into the two tins
and level surface. Bake in preheated oven for 45–50 minutes.
Loosen edges of cake and leave to
cool completely in the tin.

To decorate:
Whisk the cream, lemon juice and
icing sugar together until thick,
using half the lemon cream to
sandwich cakes together. Fill a
piping bag with the remaining
cream and pipe 11 rosettes around
the top edge of cake. Decorate
each rosette with a whole hazelnut,
and then cut the sliced lemon into
quarters and place between each
rosette.

OAT & APRICOT CRUMBLES

Filling:
*225g (8oz) 'no need to soak'
    apricots, chopped*
150ml (¼ pint) orange juice

Crumble:
175g (6oz) plain flour, sifted
175g (6oz) porridge oats
*225g (8oz) butter, chilled and
    cubed*
175g (6oz) demerara sugar
*75g (3oz) coconut chips
Icing sugar for dusting

Put the apricots and orange juice into a pan and bring to the boil. Cover and simmer gently for 5 minutes until softened. Cool. Pre-heat oven to 180C, 350F, Gas Mark 4. Grease and line the base of a 18cm x 28cm (7 inch x 11 inch) baking tin, at least 2.5cm (1 inch) deep. Put the flour and porridge oats into a large bowl, and using your fingertips rub in the cubed butter until it is evenly distributed throughout the mixture. Stir in the sugar. For the base, spoon half the mixture into the prepared tin and press down evenly with the back of a spoon. Stir the coconut chips into the remaining mixture, and spread the apricots in an even layer over the base. Then evenly sprinkle with the remaining crumble. Bake in preheated oven for about 1 hour until golden. Cool slightly then cut into 16 triangles. Dust with icing sugar, lift out with a palette knife. Can be served warm or cold. If served warm take care, as the triangles are very crumbly.

*From Health Shops, or you can use desiccated coconut.

John Heeks

We all know the saying "I'm wearing my .... hat today". Don't take this literally, as I don't mean the hat on your head, if you happen to wear one, it's the way we interpret the personas we see in public.

The first time I saw John Heeks serving behind the counter in Heeks' Grocers and Delicatessen shop, I saw a rather serious young man, with sharp blue eyes and a fresh-faced complexion. Whenever I went into the shop he always had a pleasant and attentive manner, nothing was too much trouble for him, whether reaching up to a top shelf for a tin of soup for me, or saying a quick "can I help you" if he saw me dithering by the chiller cabinet. So in effect John's hat, and this time I do literally mean "the hat on his head", was very much a shopkeeper's one, even if he hadn't been wearing one of the white trilby type hats male assistants and staff wear in supermarkets and food shops. A spotless white coat completed John's attire in the shop, and I had never seen him dressed otherwise.

We now move on to a New Year's Eve. Newcomers to Lavenham my family and I were sitting in the Angel Hotel having a meal, and celebrating the coming New Year. The restaurant was full, and idly looking round at the crowd I saw a young man detach himself from a group in a corner. He was wearing a dinner jacket and black tie, and he looked familiar, but I couldn't place where I had seen him before, yet I knew I had somewhere. He made for the back of the restaurant, disappeared into the kitchens only to reappear, like white rabbit, a few moments later. He continued to do this throughout the evening, and at the time I thought he must be the restaurant manager making periodic visits to the kitchens to ensure everything was running smoothly for the hotel's New Year's Eve customers.

Time has moved on, and I now know the sophisticated-looking, dashing young man in a dinner jacket I had seen on that particular New Year's Eve, is the son of Betty Heeks. The many trips he made to the kitchens were to see Jane, his girlfriend, who was busy working on that very busy New Year's Eve in The Angel Hotel, he also turned out to be "that nice young man" who served me in Heeks' shop!

Since John's father died some years ago he has run the family grocery shop together with his mother and sister Anne, and like most family businesses its origins go back a few generations. His grandfather started coming to Lavenham from Bury, cycling on his bicycle, selling butter from door to door, and gradually built up a steady round of customers. He was eventually able to open his own shop at No. 9 Market Place, and when he was "called up" to serve in the 1914–1918 war the business still carried on, run by John's grandmother and her sister-in-law. His grandfather then moved his shop to its present site, and was later joined by John's father in 1939, who continued to work there for the rest of his life.

When John left school there wasn't a great deal of employment in Lavenham and the surrounding area, but his father had no intention of allowing his son to become idle and, in John's own words, told him in true Suffolk dialogue "come on boy, get working in the shop, you aren't going to sit on your backside all day", and John didn't argue with him!

John has seen many changes in the shop since his grandfather and father ran the business. There is now a delicatessen and an off licence, and a wide range of speciality foods and confectionery. I asked him how many cheeses they stocked, and he told me they currently had at least 30, and that he finds it interesting to see which cheese customers favour the most; it may be a ripe Stilton or Gorgonzola, or the more milder Dolce latté.

Christmas time sees this tiny shop at its busiest, with lots to offer. It's then the off licence comes into it's own with no less than 30 Malt Whiskeys to choose from, rich, ruby red ports, and wines – reds and whites from California, France and Australia. In fact, John tells me their range is as wide and diverse as space will allow. I have sometimes heard visitors in the shop express their delight and surprise at seeing luxury items such as stem ginger in syrup, cherries and apricots in brandy, alongside chocolates from Switzerland and Belgium, and rich gourmet sauces to accompany pastas of all shapes and colours. I couldn't help thinking that although it may not be Harrods, the name of the shop *does* begin with an "H" and end with an "S", so they do have something in common, as well as both selling best quality products and giving excellent service and satisfaction to their customers.

When John's father died unexpectedly in 1983, his future took on a more definite role and pattern. A family conference was held between John, his mother Betty, and his sister Anne, and they decided to carry on running the shop between them. Anne immediately gave up her job with a local garage, where she had worked as a secretary, and became a shopkeeper with her mother and brother almost overnight. The shop and accommodation, now extended, enables each branch of the family to live conveniently side by side, with John and his family living above the shop, his mother in the adjoining house, and Anne and her family living in the end property.

So from the beginning, what originally started out as a relatively humble, but enterprising idea on the part of John's grandfather, cycling to Lavenham selling butter from door to door, then opening a small shop in the Market Place, has now grown into a small lively emporium in the heart of Lavenham's medieval village, serving its inhabitants, and the many visitors who come to visit and stay in Lavenham during the year.

After talking to John it was time to ask for some recipes for my book. I knew I would get a good response, as he is married to a real "foodie" (yes, he did marry Jane, and they now have an enchanting little girl called Katie). Jane used to run one of the local restaurants in Lavenham, called The Flame Lily, with her twin sister Sarah, and she had no shortage of recipes. These are the ones she gave to me. They make up a three-course meal for 4 people, ideal for a special occasion, and not too lavish.

DEVILLED BACON AND MUSHROOM CUPS

Serves 4

4 large thin slices of white bread
75g (3oz) melted butter
50g (2oz) small onions (shallots)
6 rashers of streaky bacon, cut
   into thin strips
225g (8oz) mushrooms, chopped
1 tbsp Worcestershire sauce
1 tsp tomato puree
Seasoning
2 tbsp sour cream
4 sprigs of chervil to garnish

Use a large biscuit cutter to stamp the bread into rounds. Soak the rounds in 50g (2oz) melted butter and fit into a tartlet tray – place an empty tray on top to hold bread in place and cook in preheated oven 200C, 400F Gas Mark 6 for 10 minutes. Take top tray off and continue to bake for a further 10 minutes until brown and crispy. Meanwhile make the filling by frying the onion and bacon in the remaining 25g (1oz) of butter until lightly browned, add the mushrooms and cook, stirring in the Worcestershire sauce, tomato puree and seasoning. Fill the toast shells and garnish with sour cream and chervil.

CHICKEN WITH LEMON & ALMOND

Serves 4

4 skinless chicken breasts
1 large onion
2 lemons
½ bottle medium white wine
75g (3oz) flaked almonds
1 dsp of fresh thyme, chopped
Chicken stock

Sauté chicken breasts on both sides in a little olive oil until brown. Add sliced onion, thyme, zest and juice of both lemons, and cook for a few minutes until onion is soft. Add the white wine and ¾ of the almonds, and then put enough chicken stock into an ovenproof dish to cover the chicken. Cook, covered, in preheated oven 200C, 400F, Gas Mark 6 for ½–¾ hour, or until chicken is cooked. Drain the juice off and reduce to help thicken sauce – you may need to thicken the sauce – if so melt a little butter 50g (2oz) in saucepan, add enough flour to make a roux, and then add the sauce a little at a time. To serve, toast remainder of the almonds, and sprinkle over the chicken, add a little double cream to the sauce, it will make all the difference!

APRICOT WHOLEWHEAT SYRUP PUDDING

Serves 4

4 tbsp golden syrup
110g (4oz) whole-wheat flour,
*   sifted*
2½ tsp baking powder
2 large eggs
Diced dried apricots (enough to
*   cover the bottom of your dish)*
110g (4oz) soft brown sugar
110g (4oz) soft margarine

You will need an 850ml (1½ pint) basin, well buttered. Place syrup and diced apricots in the base of the pudding basin. Place all the other ingredients in a bowl and beat well for 2–3 minutes, until well mixed. Spoon the mixture on top of the syrup and apricots – level out, cover with a double piece of buttered foil, pleated in the middle to allow for expansion, fold over the edges of the basin and tie down with string. Place in a steamer and steam for 1½ hours, keep a check on the water level and top up with boiling water. Serve with custard or cream; adding some good marmalade to the filling makes a lovely change, and works very well.

Sarah Boosé

Driving back to Lavenham from Earl's Colne recently, my husband and I stopped at a Farm Shop in Wickham St. Pauls. Once inside the shop we found that they not only sold fruit and vegetables, but homemade chutneys, preserves, fudge and other homemade produce. This was too good an opportunity to miss, as we are always on the lookout for homemade products to sell on the bookstall and gift shop in Lavenham's St. Peter and St. Paul Church, which my husband manages, and we have found that homemade jams and chutneys are popular "sellers".

A pleasant and attractive young lady, with light brown hair, and hazel coloured eyes, introduced herself as Sarah Boosé, and went on to tell us she worked for Spencer's Farm Shop, and that she was responsible for making all the homemade products we saw on display.

Sarah lives in Long Melford above the Old Village Stores, which, like most of the shops there, has been turned into an antique shop. Talking to Sarah and listening to what she had to say, it was obvious that here was a person who shared *my* enjoyment for cooking, and enthusiasm for working with homegrown and local produce. We didn't have long to stop and talk, but this is what Sarah told us about herself.

"I've always enjoyed cooking, and for years I have made my own jam and pickles for home use. I began making chutneys and pickles for sale to the public in 1997, starting in a very small way, and learning by trial and error – not without the occasional disaster! Over the years I have streamlined my methods of production, but I am still very much a 'home industry'. Each variety is handmade in small batches, using local produce wherever possible. My products are sold by local farm shops, pubs and at farmers' markets.

"I am employed at Spencer's Farm Shop in Wickham St. Pauls, Essex, where we offer a variety of homegrown fruit, vegetables and other local produce. Our season and homegrown produce starts in April with early asparagus, and continues throughout the summer with a wide range of soft fruit and vegetables, both 'ready picked' and P.Y.O. and then into the winter with a choice and variety of apples.

I'm a firm believer in home cooking with fresh produce. Working and cooking doesn't give me much time for making elaborate meals, but here are two of my favourite recipes. The Pumpkin Pie is a good way of using pumpkin flesh up after making Halloween lanterns!"

COURGETTE BAKE

Serves 2

2–3 large courgettes
1 large onion, chopped
1 garlic clove crushed
110g (4oz) Cheddar or strong
   flavoured cheese, grated
1 tsp sugar
110g (4oz) mushrooms, trimmed
   and sliced
1 small can (227g) plum tomatoes
1 tbsp tomato puree
Pinch of Italian seasoning or
   Italian Cube
Olive oil

Wash and trim courgettes, leaving skin on. Slice lengthways and cook until just soft in boiling salted water, drain well. Fry onions, garlic and mushrooms in olive oil until soft, but not coloured. Prepare tomato sauce by heating tomatoes, add sugar, Italian seasoning, and salt and pepper to taste. Grease an ovenproof dish, layer courgettes with onion and mushroom mixture. Pour a little sauce and sprinkle some cheese over each layer. Top with remaining sauce and cheese, and bake in a preheated oven, 180C, 350F, Gas Mark 4 until the cheese bubbles and turns golden brown. Serve immediately with crusty bread.

TEXAS STYLE PUMPKIN PIE

Serves 6

225g (8oz) pkt Digestive biscuits
110g (4oz) butter
225g (8oz) caster sugar
1 sachet gelatine
3 egg yolks, beaten
3 egg whites
225g (8oz) cooked (or canned)
   pumpkin
1 tsp ground cinnamon
¼ tsp salt
¼ tsp ground nutmeg
125ml (4floz) whipping cream
110g (4oz) toasted coconut
200ml (7½floz) milk

Crush biscuits, melt butter and combine. Press firmly into a greased and lined 23cm (9 inch) loose bottom flan tin, and allow to set.

In a large saucepan combine 175g (6oz) sugar, gelatine, cinnamon, salt and nutmeg. Mix egg yolks with milk and add to gelatine mixture. Cook, stirring constantly, until mixture thickens slightly. Stir in pumpkin, chill until nearly set. Whisk egg whites until soft peaks form, add remaining sugar and whisk until stiff. Fold egg whites into pumpkin mixture, turn into biscuit crust and chill until firm. To serve, turn out of tin onto serving dish, sprinkle with toasted coconut. Whip cream and pipe round edge, or serve separately.

Rosemary Wheeler

A dainty diminutive figure, slim ankles perched on fashionable high-heeled shoes, wearing a colourful, silky flowered dress, with an eye-catching frothy concoction perched on her head, gloves and handbag to match, and looking every inch as if she was on her way to a Garden Party, instead of just having driven over from Cambridge, where she now lives, on a particularly hot day, to read the lesson in Church. This was my first impression of Rosemary Wheeler, and never mind about "ladies who lunch" and "ladies who take tea", this lady was definitely one "who wore hats" and wore them with chic and style.

Do not be deceived by what you see, this is a strong capable woman of many talents. Ask Rosemary to speak at any gathering or function, and she will deliver an interesting and articulate talk on the history of Lavenham and its people, and holds the L.A.M.D.A. Gold Medal for Public Speaking. An accomplished pianist, she played the organ for services in Lavenham's beautiful church for many years, and is much sought after to play the piano at social gatherings and concerts in Cambridge, accompanied by a singer, songs from Gilbert and Sullivan, Opera and Oratorio are among her repertoire. She learnt the butchering trade from her father as soon as she left school, and grew up in an age when hard work was commonplace, and one respected and never questioned their parent's authority.

Family butcher's shops are now few and far between in villages and small towns, and large supermarkets have encroached on their trade, some would say this is called progress, but others may disagree. Lavenham still has its family butcher's shop, which is the same shop where Rosemary was born and grew up in, and although she has moved away she still retains close links with Lavenham.

This is Rosemary's story of her early years in Lavenham, as she remembers it..........

"I was born at No.1 High Street, Lavenham, above the butcher's shop opposite the Swan Hotel, in the same room where my father had been born thirty years earlier. My grandfather, Edward Wheeler, had taken over the butcher's shop in 1894, and when he died in 1926, my father, Harry Victor Wheeler, became the owner.

"I left school at the age of fifteen, and joined the family business. It was wartime, and with father's staff being called-up to do National Service, and my brother, a few years my senior, also awaiting his call-up papers, Dad needed someone to train and help in the shop, and who better than his daughter. I was pleased to do this, as I hated school, and to be able to leave a year earlier, suited me very well. During my last year at school I only attended Monday to Thursday, as I had to help with delivering meat in the villages surrounding Lavenham, every Friday. We left home with a van laden with orders at 7am, and returned home eleven hours later, a very long day, and no overtime pay in those days either! On Saturdays we delivered to other villages from 7am until 2.30pm.

"When I joined the business full-time, I soon discovered there was far more to butchering than just delivering the meat. I had to learn how to use knives, choppers and saws. My hands had to get used to very hot soda water, it was all we had in those days to 'scrub up' the blood and grease in a butcher's shop – detergents weren't even heard of then.

"I helped to make sausages and brawn, and learnt how to sharpen a knife correctly. I also helped in the slaughterhouse, and was shown how to clean and dress the animals once they had been killed. Slaughtering methods have changed vastly over the years. When my father first started, he killed animals by the poleaxe method, which must have been quite a terrifying experience – I still have his poleaxe! By the time I was involved, a small gun, called a humane killer, was used.

"When the carcass of a bullock, pig or lamb was on the block in the shop, I was able to chop, saw and cut it into sections for window display and, eventually, into joints for customers – a job I particularly liked doing.

"As it was wartime, I had to understand rationing procedures, and how little – and believe me it was little – each person was allowed each week. At the very worst times during the war, the ration was reduced to ten pence (10d) each week. Although brisket of beef was only eight pence (8d) a pound, and fillet steak one shilling and sixpence (1/6d), it meant that a person on their own could only have about half a pound of fillet steak for the whole week. I have never been able to understand why it was, that for every other commodity rationed during the war, only meat was rationed by the money's worth, as all other food was rationed by weight – 2ozs cheese, butter, bacon, sugar etc. There must have been a good reason, but I have never been able to find out what it was.

"I was also taught how to bone and roll a joint. Customers sometimes liked the bone removed from a rib of beef or sirloin, as they felt it was easier to carve, but I feel that a lot of the flavour is lost when the bone is removed.

"I became the third generation in the Wheeler family – my grandmother, Martha Wheeler, had helped in the shop, as did my mother, Gertrude Wheeler, who also delivered meat by horse and trap, in the days before my father owned a van. From 1943 to 1950 I spent seven years as a woman butcher, an unusual job for a woman in those days, and even in these days of so called 'equality', there are very few real women butchers around.

"Since moving away from Lavenham I now lead a very different life, but come back as often as I can to see friends and attend church, and I love entertaining and cooking. Prime British Beef – a rib with the bone left in – is still top of my list, and you can't beat it for flavour."

I couldn't agree more, and now it was time to ask Rosemary for some recipes.........

PORK AND SAGE PARCELS

Serves 4

4 thick loin pork chops or steaks
50g (2oz) butter
225g (8oz) mushrooms, cleaned
   and thinly sliced
1 tbsp flour
Juice of 1 lemon
Freshly ground black pepper
2 tbsp chopped fresh sage
150ml (¼ pint) double cream

Heat butter in pan and brown pork quickly. Remove and place on individual pieces of foil. Sprinkle with pepper and chopped sage on each chop. Fry the mushrooms in the butter for 3 minutes, then sprinkle in the flour and stir thoroughly. Add lemon juice and mix in thoroughly for 1–2 minutes. Divide the mushroom mixture between the four chops. Pour two tbsp of cream over each chop and seal the parcels securely. Bake in preheated oven for about 1 hour at 170C, 325F, Gas Mark 3. Serve with mashed potatoes and green peas.

POT ROAST BRISKET WITH ROOT VEGETABLES

Serves 6

1½kg (3lb5oz) rolled brisket
4 carrots, cleaned and scraped
6 small onions
3 turnips, peeled
5 sticks celery, cleaned
1 small swede, peeled
Beef dripping or vegetable oil
225g (8oz) mushrooms, peeled
300ml (½ pint) rich stock
1 bay leaf
2 sprigs of thyme
Freshly ground black pepper
Salt

Cut turnips and swede into small chunks. Chop the carrots into large chunks and cut celery into 2.5cm (1 inch) pieces. Peel onions and leave whole. Put oil into thick cooking casserole and heat. Sear and brown the joint, take out and set aside. Put prepared vegetables into pan and lightly brown them, remove vegetables and set aside. Empty oil from casserole, then put back the meat with the vegetables and mushrooms around it. Add the stock, bay leaf and thyme. Season to taste. Cover with lid and bring to simmering point. Then put into preheated oven 140C, 275F, Gas Mark 1 and cook for 3½–4 hours. Serve with jacket potato and creamed cabbage.

ENGLISH LAMB WITH ASPARAGUS

Serves 6

1½kg (3lb5oz) shoulder meat cut
    into 5cm (2") chunks.
1kg (2¼lb) fresh asparagus
75g (3oz) butter
6 small onions, peeled and
    chopped
300ml (½ pint) double cream
Lemon juice
Ground black pepper and salt

Wash, scrape and cook asparagus in lightly salted water until tender. Drain well and reserve cooking liquid and asparagus tips. Liquidise the remaining stems, using a little of the cooking liquid, then sieve to get rid of stringy pieces. Trim fat from the lamb and toss into seasoned flour. Brown in deep frying pan with melted butter and onions. When nicely browned gradually stir in 300ml (½ pint) of asparagus liquid to make a thickish sauce. Cover the pan and simmer meat for an hour, skimming off any fat. When meat has cooked, and sauce reduced, add the asparagus puree and the cream. Add seasoning and lemon juice. Serve with boiled potatoes and the asparagus tips.

Margaret Morley

When I first met Margaret she reminded me of my headmistress of many years ago, and I immediately put her into the teaching category, but no, Margaret was a farmer's wife, widowed and living in Lavenham. With her silvery hair immaculately coiffured into a chignon, upright bearing, and a pair of unwavering blue eyes, that looked down at you quizzically when you first met her, you knew she was not one to suffer fools gladly!

But there's another side to Margaret, and when you get to know her you appreciate her quick wit, and dry sense of humour, behind the headmistress look those blue eyes can twinkle with amusement when something has amused her. Always impeccably dressed, she would not look out of place chairing a 'Women of the Year' luncheon, which is held at the Savoy Hotel in London each year.

Margaret's story is a farming one, she married Philip Morley, a farmer, in 1949, and first went to live in the pretty village of Shimpling, and then moving to Sicklesmere, before finally settling down in Cockfield which lies between Lavenham and Bury St. Edmunds. Married life started off with none of today's 'mod cons', and although the farmhouse was in pleasant surroundings, it did not have water, electricity or sanitation. Water was fetched by Margaret's husband from a neighbouring water pump or well, and brought home in large milk churns. Oil lamps had to be dealt with each day, and their wicks cut and trimmed. Rooms that were in daily use had open fires, and grates had to be raked out, and fireplace surrounds black-leaded and polished daily until they were gleaming.

Like most housewives in the late 40s and early 50s, Margaret was kept fully occupied bringing up her two sons, looking after her husband and keeping house generally, but as time went by she was expected to help on the farm, and had to muck in and help with the hoeing of sugar beet, a very back-breaking job, and among other numerous farming chores there was the daily feeding of young calves, rearing and looking after the chickens and hens, and eggs sold at the door or taken to market, were then considered to be a farmer's wife's 'perks', which helped to swell their finances and Margaret's housekeeping.

A weekly bake was usually on a Friday, when jam tarts, buns and fruit cakes, would be made to last the week, and like most housewives in those days Margaret always made sure there was something in the cake tin to offer unexpected callers with their cup of tea.

The main meal of the day was dinner, which was served midday. In the Morley household there was always something substantial for this meal, such as rabbit or pigeon pie, steak and kidney pudding, with a fruit pie to follow to satisfy the hungry family and workers. On Sundays there would be roast beef and Yorkshire pudding with plenty of homegrown vegetables from the garden.

Rabbits can be bought easily these days, already packed and jointed, from butchers and supermarkets, but in those days, farmers and their workers went on shoots (and probably still do) bringing home rabbits for their wives to cook, but they also had to be skinned, cleaned and jointed. Rabbit pie was a great family favourite with the Morley family, and as in most farming families, recipes are handed down from generation to generation. Before I left Margaret I made sure she gave me her rabbit pie, and date and walnut bread recipes, as well as *her special apple pie*!

RABBIT PIE

1 rabbit cleaned and jointed (get
  your butcher to do this or buy a
  pre-packed jointed one from a
  supermarket)
2 slices of bacon
1 hard-boiled egg (optional)
3 level tbsp chopped parsley
1 large onion, chopped
2 level tbsp flour
1 level tsp salt
½ tbsp chopped sage
½ tsp black pepper
600ml (1pt) stock (beef or
  vegetable cube)
175g (6oz) rough puff pastry (or
  short-crust) (ready made is
  easier)

Mix together flour, salt and pepper on a plate, and cover rabbit with this mixture. Place joints with onion in a saucepan, add 600ml (1pt) stock and simmer on hot plate for 1½ hours. When cooked turn into pie-dish to cool. Add sliced egg, bacon, chopped parsley and chopped sage. Roll out rough puff pastry at least 2.5cm (1 inch) larger than your pie dish. Cut a strip off all round, and lay it on the wet edge of the pie-dish with the cut edge outside. Brush this with milk and put the remainder of the pastry on top. Trim edges using a sharp knife. Ornament top with leaves of pastry from trimmings. Glaze by brushing with milk or yolk of an egg. Bake in pre-heated oven 190C, 375F, Gas Mark 5 for 20–30 minutes until pastry is well risen and golden brown. Serves 4 generous portions with vegetables of your choice.

APPLE PIE

Serves 4–6

225g (8oz) shortcrust pastry
1kg (1¼lb) cooking apples
A little grated lemon rind
Enough sugar to sweeten (about
  2–3 tbsp)
2 cloves (optional)

Peel, core and slice apples. Place in pie dish with sugar and sprinkle with water. Roll out the pastry a little larger than the pie dish, cut off a strip about ½ inch wide. Damp the edges of the dish and cover with the strip, damp this pastry and cover with the remainder, being careful not to stretch the pastry. Glaze pastry by brushing with the white of an egg, or with water and sugar. Bake in pre-heated oven 200C, 400F, Gas Mark 6 for 20–25 minutes. When cooked sprinkle with icing sugar. Serves 4–6.

DATE AND WALNUT BREAD

225g (8oz) self-raising flour
1 level tsp bicarbonate powder
50g (2oz) caster sugar
1 egg
25g (1oz) margarine
50g (2oz) chopped walnuts
350g (12oz) chopped dates
150ml (¼pt) water

Sieve dry ingredients together. Put sugar, margarine and dates into a saucepan and pour over boiling water. Stir well and leave to cool. Then add rest of ingredients and mix well. Put into a large loaf tin 23cm x 12.5cm (9" x 5"), greased and floured and bake in preheated oven 190C–200C, 375F–400F, Gas Mark 5–6 for approximately 50–55 minutes. Leave in tin for 5 minutes then turn out on wire tray to cool. This bread keeps well and is delicious spread with butter.

Win Gage

Approaching Monks Eleigh from Ipswich, and nestling in the brow of a hill, is a craft shop and tea room. Here you will find Win Gage, a tall slim lady in her early fifties, with a neatly bobbed and fringed hair style, framing a calm, untroubled face, masking a firmness of purpose, which enabled this enterprising lady to embark and make a success of a craft shop and tea room. A band of cheerful ladies, some have worked with Win for 20 years, serve morning coffee, lunches and teas, and are responsible for preparing freshly cooked meals, which are listed on a blackboard by the counter, throughout the day. Freshly cooked food usually means you may have to queue and wait, but that doesn't deter the number of people parking their cars daily in Win's car park; proof that this is a good place to eat, and if you have to wait, well the food and service is worth waiting for!

All kinds of gifts such as books, jewellery, glassware, pictures, jams and cordials are on display, and many other things to tempt you to open your purse and spend your money. Across the courtyard is the Flower and Corn Dolly Shop, where roses, snowdrops and anemones are displayed in a profusion of colour against a background of the traditional corn and maize dollies, which were sold in the original Corn Craft Shop formed in 1976. These are made in many shapes and forms, and the Suffolk Horseshoe is one of the most attractive and popular to be sold in the shop. Here you can buy silk flowers to make your own flower arrangement, or you can watch Sandra making one of her stunning silken flower arrangements. It's fascinating to see her twisting petals and foliage into crescents and shapes of all sizes. Containers of brilliant red and orange poppies vie with delicate shades of pink and cream roses, baskets are filled to the brim with green foliage and grasses, and there is an abundance of flowers all temptingly displayed in vases, so very few people walk out of the flower shop without buying something from this display and profusion of colour.

Win has a success story to tell, but one not without its trials and tribulations, showing a steeliness of purpose and achievement.........

"I trained as a nurse, and thought that would be my vocation in life, but marrying into a farming family led me in another direction, and I became involved in the family's arable and poultry farm business. As a hobby I got interested in making corn dollies, which was a family tradition, and had been practised on the farm for many years. We began by selling them by the farm gate, and soon sold out, finding that people came back again to buy more, and that is how the idea of opening a shop selling corn dollies began. After a while I had an idea to create a tea room where people could sit in natural, welcoming, and homely surroundings, eat fresh home cooked food, and wander round a craft shop, browsing and choosing gifts at their leisure.

"On a visit to America my tea room idea was further fuelled, when travelling around I saw that the tea rooms over there were bright, with a homespun, rustic look about them, tables and chairs were in pine, water colour paintings were on the walls, and they were always busy and full with customers. I couldn't wait to get home to turn my idea of opening a tea room into a reality. The derelict farm buildings which used to store corn, were gradually restored, and have now been turned into a flower shop. The actual site of the shop and tea room was originally a corn mill, where corn used to be ground to feed the farm's chickens and poultry, and is now known as the Corn Craft Shop and Tea Room.

"We are open all the year round except on Christmas Day and Boxing Day, and the business has grown and expanded since the original Corn Craft Shop was formed and opened in 1976. Running the craft shop and tea room takes up most of my time, but I can't imagine doing anything else, and when I look around the tea room and see customers relaxed, happy and enjoying their food in surroundings which were once just an idea in my head, I know I have realised my ambition to open a cosy tea room in a *'little corner of England'*, just like the tearooms I saw in *America*, where *they* resembled a *'little corner of England'*!"

Some favourites from the Corn Craft's blackboard!

CHICKEN AND VEGETABLE SOUP

Makes 1.2 litres (2 pints)

Carcass of one chicken
110g (4oz) of meat from chicken
1 medium carrot
Half a medium onion
1 stick of celery
Half a small parsnip
1 quarter of swede
Half a small turnip
2 large potatoes
*Seasoning: pepper and salt, and a
    few mixed herbs*
2 Knorr chicken stock cubes

Boil carcass of chicken, saving 110g (4oz) of meat. Chop all vegetables and place in stock plus water to make up 1.2lts (2 pints) of fluid. Add a sprinkling of mixed herbs and the stock cubes. Bring to the boil and simmer for 40 mins. Season with salt and pepper to taste. Coarsely mash the vegetables to thicken the soup, but leaving a few pieces to give texture. Add the chopped up pieces of chicken and simmer for a further 10 mins. Serve piping hot with crusty bread or rolls.

CHICKEN AND HERB PASTA

Serves 6

1 large chopped onion
50g (2oz) butter
3 tbsp plain flour
Pepper and salt to taste
1.2ltrs–1.5ltrs (2–3 pints) of milk
*1 dessertspoon chopped mixed
    herbs*
*225g (8oz) chopped cooked
    chicken*
*175g (6oz) freshly cooked tricolour
    pasta shells*
Sliced tomato
Breadcrumbs
25g (1oz) grated cheese

Fry the onion in butter, add seasoning and flour. Slowly add milk to make a creamy sauce (not too thick). Add chicken, herbs and pasta. Turn into a large dish. Decorate with sliced tomato, sprinkle with breadcrumbs and grated cheese. Brown gently under grill.

LEMON MERINGUE PIE

Serves 6

Pastry:
75g (3oz) butter
175g (6oz) plain flour
Pinch salt
1 tsp caster sugar
1 egg yolk
Cold water to mix

Rub butter into flour, add salt and stir in sugar and mix to a pliable dough with egg yolk and water.

Knead lightly, roll out into a round and line 20cm (8 inch) flan tin. Place a piece of greaseproof on top and then add dried rice to keep the pastry level and bake blind at 170C, 325F, Gas Mark 3 for 10 mins. Remove rice and paper and bake for a further 10 minutes or until cooked.

Filling:
2 lemons
300ml (½pt) water
75g (3oz) sugar

40g (1½oz) cornflour
2 egg yolks

Blend cornflour with a little water to a smooth cream. Heat remaining water, grated lemon rind and juice. Stir in cornflour and bring to the boil, stirring all the time. Cook for 2 minutes then remove from heat. Stir in sugar and egg yolks to make a smooth mixture. Leave to cool and then pour into pastry case.

Meringue:
2 egg whites
110g (4oz) caster sugar

Whisk egg whites until stiff. Whisk in half the sugar a little at a time, then fold in the remainder. Spread over lemon filling right to the edge and swirl attractively. Bake for a further 35–40 mins. at 150C, 300F, Gas Mark 2.

CARAMEL SLICE

Shortbread base:
175g (6oz) butter
75g (3oz) caster sugar
275g (10oz) plain flour
50g (2oz) ground rice

Cream butter and sugar together. Gradually add flour and ground rice (mixture should be crumbly). Spread mixture into a lined Swiss roll tin 30cm x 20cm (12 inches x 8.5 inches). Press the mixture down until level and smooth. Prick with a fork and bake at 160C, 325F, Gas Mark 3 for 25–30 minutes.

Caramel:
110g (4oz) butter
2 level tbsp caster sugar
2 tbsp golden syrup
1 med. tin condensed milk

Place all ingredients into a strong saucepan and slowly melt and bring to the boil, stirring all the time. Gently boil for 10–15 minutes until the caramel looks a rich golden brown. Pour onto shortbread and spread evenly. When cold, melt 225g (8oz) of dark chocolate and spread onto the caramel. Leave to set and then cut into squares.

Meinir and Dewi Owen and the Story Behind 'direct Welsh Lamb'

Anyone who knows me realises I have a soft spot for farmers, perhaps having married one who left farming many years ago, it's not surprising. However, farming today has changed; instead of taking their cattle to market for auction, a lot of farmers have found, through marketing a traditional product and using innovative advertising methods, they can sell their meat direct to the public.

I love going around the farmers' markets in the Suffolk area, these are held each month, and are the places to go to buy first class reared lamb, pork and beef. One of the advantages of buying meat direct from farmers is that you know where it comes from, you can talk to the farmer, and you can always get best quality meat, and good value for your money.

Dewi and his wife Meinir, have lived at the family farm for 13 years, having taken it over from Dewi's parents. They have three girls, Carys 19, who is at University studying accountancy, Bethan who is 17 and studying for her 'A' Levels, Rhian is 13, and following the family tradition, with a keen interest in farming. They keep cattle, suckler calves and sheep, and Meinir has a full-time job working as a 'cook in charge' at the local primary school, which caters for 200 pupils. A hard working couple, who in spite of the agriculture recession in 1998, have not let this setback dampen their enthusiasm for farming, and were determined to survive.

Their story is set in Wales where Welsh lamb is brought up on the sweet grasses of the Welsh mountains. The company is called 'direct Welsh Lamb Ltd.' and was set up in June 1999, when five members got together to form a co-operative, so they could sell their lamb direct to the public through mail order.

The idea of setting up the company came from Dewi Owen in 1998 at a time when agriculture was at an all-time low. Dewi has been buying lambs for abattoirs since 1976, and had many contacts, suppliers and buyers.

He started talking to local farmers about the idea of selling local Welsh lamb direct from Aberdovey, and they agreed to supply the lamb.

The rest of the team come from a variety of backgrounds, Meirion Roberts is a main supplier, and set up direct Welsh Lamb's website from his own company Dragon Systems. Aled Rees is a farmer, and following government advice for farmers to diversify, has sold off part of his farm to buy the Penmaendyfi hotel near Aberdovey in North Wales. Idris Evans is a full time farmer, and his wife Mari looks after the company's finances. Dewi's wife Meinir is the company's secretary, and Gwyn Evans the marketing adviser.

Their company has since grown from strength to strength with increasing demand for their top quality Welsh Lamb, and was recently voted the best tasting lamb in Wales on HTV's 'Grassroots' programme in a competition involving three other leading Welsh lamb suppliers.

The very best of Welsh lamb is now available 'freezer ready' and delivered direct to the doorstep throughout the U.K. This is all down to the marketing initiative of a group of farmers living in mid Wales who, when faced with the crisis in agriculture, set up their own mail order lamb business to increase farm incomes and give consumers a better deal into the bargain. The initiative of Dewi and the farmers in the Dyfi Estuary is beginning to pay off, and through marketing a traditional product, using innovative advertising methods, direct Welsh Lamb looks set to be a recipe for success.

Lamb figures high in the Owen kitchen, and Meinir has given me these three main course recipes, using succulent, boneless cuts of lamb, followed by a delicious Apple Crumble.

HERBY PENMAEN LAMB

Serves 4–6

1 shoulder of Welsh Lamb boned
  (keep bones for stock)
900g (2lb) leeks, topped and tailed
1 medium onion, peeled and
  chopped
450g (1lb) carrots, scraped and
  peeled
1.35kg (3lb) potatoes, peeled
2 cups of vegetable stock
Few sprigs of rosemary
Few sprigs of mint, chopped
Salt and pepper

Sprinkle the inside of joint with salt and pepper, mint, rosemary and chopped onion. Tie very tightly with string. Place on roasting tray. To prepare the terrine, put leeks, carrots and potatoes through a good processor on the thin blade so they are sliced very thinly like crisps. Put a layer of potatoes in a buttered dish, then a layer of leeks then carrots and so on until you end up with a layer of potatoes. Season in between each layer with salt and pepper. Press down firmly, then fill to top with vegetable stock. It should be about 8cm (3 inches) thick. Place the lamb on top tray of oven and vegetable terrine on lower shelf. Cook at 200C, 400F, Gas Mark 6 until the stock has been absorbed by the vegetables for about 2–2½ hours.

When cooked take a slice of the vegetables and place in the middle of a warm plate. Remove the string from the lamb and cut into slices. Place two or three slices of lamb on top of terrine, garnish with baked shallots and baby carrots and serve with mint gravy.

SWEET ESGAIR LAMB

Serves 4–6

2kg (4½lb) shoulder of Welsh lamb, boned
1 clove garlic, peeled and halved
Salt and freshly ground black pepper
225g (8oz) dried apricots
2 stalks of celery
4 tbsp set honey
1 tsp dried marjoram
2 sprigs of rosemary
2 medium slices of bread
4 tbsp fresh orange juice
1 tbsp of flour
425ml (¾ pint) chicken stock or dry red wine

Rub the garlic clove inside the cavity left by the bone, sprinkle a little salt over the outside of the joint, and set it aside while you prepare the stuffing. Roughly chop the apricots and slice the celery, then mix these ingredients with 3 tbsp of honey and the marjoram. Chop the leaves from the rosemary and add to the stuffing. Place bread in a bowl, sprinkle over large cup of milk and set aside for 2 minutes. Break up the soaked bread and mix it into the stuffing. Stir to combine the ingredients and add seasoning. Press the stuffing into the cavity and sew up a neat parcel. Place the lamb in a roasting tin. Mix the remaining honey with the orange juice and brush a little over the lamb. Roast the joint in a hot oven (200C, 400F, Gas Mark 6) for 15 minutes, then reduce the temperature to 180C, 350F, Gas Mark 4 and cook for a further 1½–1¾ hours, baste the joint frequently. Remove the meat from the tin and prepare gravy with stock or red wine.

SPICY MAETHLON LAMB

Serves 4–6

900g (2lb) fillet end of leg of lamb
1 tbsp oil
25g (1oz) butter
2 medium size onions, peeled and sliced
1 clove garlic, peeled and chopped
1 tbsp plain flour
1 tsp ground cumin seed
½ tsp ground allspice
1 tbsp tomato puree
300ml–425ml (½–¾ pint) stock
Salt and pepper to season

Cut the meat off the bone and cut into chunks. Heat the oil in pan, add the butter, and when foaming, brown the meat, a few pieces at a time. Remove the meat, add the onions and garlic and cook slowly for 5 minutes, stirring from time to time; dust in the flour and spices and continue cooking for a further 3–4 minutes. Stir in tomato puree and 300ml (½ pint) of stock, away from heat, and blend until mixture is smooth. Return pan to stove and stir mixture until boiling, reduce the heat, add the meat to pan, cover and cook for 45–60 mins. on top of stove or in oven at 180C, 350F, Gas Mark 4. Stir the mixture occasionally, adding the reserved stock if necessary and season to taste. Serve with pilaf rice and green salad.

APPLE CRUMBLE

Serves 4–6

900g (2lb) peeled, cored and
   sliced apples
110g (4oz) caster sugar
1 tsp cinnamon
2 tbsp water

Crumble topping:
225g (8oz) plain flour
75g (3oz) butter
110g (4oz) light muscovado sugar
50g (2oz) crushed cornflakes

Cook apples with sugar, cinnamon in 2 tbsp of water until soft. Set aside in overnproof dish until required. Rub butter into flour until it resembles fine breadcrumbs, add sugar and crushed cornflakes. Sprinkle topping evenly over apples. Cook in oven at 180C, 350F, Gas Mark 4 for 30–40 minutes. Serve with homemade piping hot custard.

Pam Gray

Last summer my daughter and I were touring around the Norfolk countryside, looking for somewhere to stop for tea. It was one of those boiling hot days, when all you want to do is to collapse into a chair and drink a refreshing cup of tea. We finally stopped at the small picturesque village of Castle Acre, and almost next to the village church was the lovely 18th century oak beamed Willow Cottage Tea Rooms, run by Pam and Barry Gray. The tea rooms were full, so we sat outside at tables under shady umbrellas. The tea was delicious, and I sampled some fragrantly scented Lavender Cake, whilst Belinda ordered a slice of the Triple Decker Chocolate Gateaux.

Pam came out, sat at our table and chatted to us. She told us that as well as running the tearooms, they also did bed and breakfast, and have 2 double and 2 twin rooms for letting, and were gradually building up a thriving business. Running the tea rooms was a complete change for both of them, Pam having worked in a bank in Kent and Barry involved in stock broking in the City, but both of them seem to have taken to it like ducks to water.

Luckily neither of them are strangers to cooking, and Pam is adamant that "we won't serve anything we haven't tried and enjoyed ourselves". Their lunch menu is extensive with homemade soups, omelettes, sandwiches and baked potatoes, all with a good selection of fillings. Good "old-fashioned puds" like Treacle Pudding, Spotted Dick, Crumbles, Fruit Pies and Bread & Butter Pudding regularly appear on the Gray's lunchtime menu board, and are firm favourites with customers, even during the hot summer months, when they offer cold desserts like Cheesecake, Lemon Meringue Pie or fresh strawberries and cream.

Customers often ask Pam for her recipes, and one family who were staying in a rented cottage in the village came in regularly each day for tea, and became addicted to their lemon cake, so much so they ordered eight slices at one sitting, but Pam only had four slices left, but said it would be on the menu the next day, so they promptly ordered eight slices for the following afternoon, which was the last day of their holiday.

Pam is always happy to pass recipes on to customers who ask for them, and I came away with some of the Willow Cottage Tea Room favourites, and have included them here in my book; I also made a mental note not to leave it too long before I returned to sample some more of the Tea Room's delicious Lavender Cake!

COURGETTE & CUMIN SOUP

Serves 4

25g (1oz) butter
1 onion, finely chopped
1 clove garlic, crushed
1 level tsp cumin
150g (5oz) potatoes, diced
350g (12oz) courgettes, sliced
   thickly (reserve a few slices for
   garnish)
450ml (¾pt) vegetable stock
300ml (½pt) milk
Salt and freshly ground black
   pepper

Melt the butter in a large saucepan and gently fry the chopped onion and crushed garlic until soft. Add the cumin and cook for 2–3 minutes. Add the diced potato, sliced courgette and stock, and cook until the vegetables are tender. Liquidize the mixture and return to the saucepan. Add the ground pepper and salt, if required. Add the milk and heat through (do not boil). Serve and garnish with sliced courgette.

PARSNIP & APPLE SOUP

Serves 6–8

25g (1oz) butter
700g (1½lb) parsnips, peeled and
   chopped
1 Bramley cooking apple, peeled
   and chopped
1½ litres (2pts) vegetable stock
½ tsp dried sage
2 cloves
150ml (¼pt) single cream
Salt and freshly ground black
   pepper

Melt butter in a large pan. Add the parsnips and apple, then cover and cook gently for 10 minutes, stirring occasionally. Add the stock, sage and cloves. Bring to the boil, cover and simmer for 30 minutes. Remove the cloves, leave to cool slightly, then puree in blender. Return to the saucepan and reheat gently with the cream. Season to taste. Serve hot, garnished with croutons or parsley.

LEMON DRIZZLE CAKE

This recipe makes three cakes, so you can eat one, and freeze the other two.

450g (1lb) soft margarine
400g (14oz) caster sugar
560g (1lb4oz) self-raising flour
8 eggs
Grated rind of 3–4 lemons
8 tbsp lemon curd
Juice from 3–4 lemons

Grease and flour 3 x 2lb loaf tins.

Cream margarine and sugar, beat in eggs, lemon curd and grated rind, then add flour. Bake for 45 minutes to 1 hour at 150C, 300F, Gas Mark 2 on middle shelf of oven. Blend lemon juice and 6–8 tbsps caster sugar. When cooked and still warm, pour mixture evenly over cakes, and allow to cool in tins.

QUEEN MOTHER CAKE

75g (3oz) soft margarine
225g (8oz) caster sugar
275g (10oz) plain flour
1 egg, beaten
1 tsp vanilla essence
1 tsp baking powder
½ tsp salt
50g (2oz) chopped walnuts
225g (8oz) chopped dates
1 tsp bicarbonate soda

Pour ¾ mug of boiling water over chopped dates, add bicarbonate of soda, let it stand while the remaining ingredients are mixed. Combine all ingredients and bake in a 23cm x 30cm (9 x 12in) greased tin at 150C, 300F, Gas Mark 2 for about 1 hr, until springy and cooked through. Allow to cool in tin. Mix 5 tbsp brown sugar, 2 tbsp butter and 2 tbsp cream and boil for 3 minutes, remove cake from tin and spread on the top of cake, then sprinkle with chopped walnuts.

LAVENDER CAKE

225g (8oz) margarine
225g (8oz) caster sugar
275g (10oz) self-raising flour
2 tsp baking powder
4 eggs
4 tbsps milk
2 heaped tsps lavender seeds

Pre-heat oven to 180C, 350F, Gas Mark 4. Cream margarine and sugar, add beaten eggs, fold in flour and baking powder and finally milk and lavender seeds. Put into greased and floured 23cm x 30 cm (9 x 12in) tin and bake for approximately 35 to 40 minutes. Then ice with lavender coloured icing, or white icing decorated with lavender coloured icing. This cake cuts into 12 generous portions.

Sally and Robert Bendall

Sally and Robert Bendall were both brought up on farms. They met 20 years ago at Chadacre College when Robert was on the staff and Sally was a student. After they married a couple of years later they set up in business rearing calves near Ipswich, living in a caravan on the site.

As there was no possibility of building a house there, they moved their caravan to Semer and rented 10 acres from Robert's father. They continued rearing calves and Robert, the green-fingered member of the family, began growing vegetables, and selling them from a table at the roadside, as well as eggs.

It was a difficult time, especially as the bottom fell out of the calf-rearing market, but the roadside selling was doing well and they continued living in the caravan for five years. Vegetable sales graduated from the roadside table to a six-foot by eight-foot hut, and within a few more years the calf business had gone completely – and finally, so had the caravan, and they were able to move into their newly built bungalow.

Sally has a large farmhouse-style kitchen where there is plenty of farming activity going on, not least the incubator, which sits just to the left of the Aga. Sally describes it as her new toy and says it is never empty, and likes to "mess around" with the different breeds of animals and poultry. Eggs from her free-range flock of Buff Orpingtons are on sale in the shop, and free-range means precisely that where Sally's hens are concerned.

The shop has now grown into a large and spacious complex of buildings, the retailing area as big as council planners will allow, and is rather like a "mini super-market" selling everything from meat and vegetables to wine and beer. Their livestock is currently 25 beef cattle, 30 pigs, three sheep – although there are more in the spring, as well as geese, chickens and turkeys.

Their hard work has paid off and their business is a front-runner in farm retailing in Britain. This keen pair have both made several trips across the Atlantic to gather ideas, and although both have been born into farming, retailing needs completely different skills (and here I speak from experience, as when I first met my husband he was farming in Somerset, and at 34 years of age decided to go into retailing, which at the time was quite a transition).

Sally and Robert now employ 12 full and part-time staff, and living on site 24 hours a day means they are rarely off duty. Their daily life is busy from 6.00am onwards, but they do try to manage a week's holiday a year with their children Tom (12), Angharad (9) and Shan (7). But as Sally is quick to point out, although they have a hard working way of life, it's in an environment many would envy.

With a family of five to feed the Aga comes in useful for Sally's baking, and with plenty of home produced food the family are, as you would expect, very well fed. Here are three recipes which are enjoyed by the Bendall family starting with baked ham, which is enriched with 'Old Growler'.

BAKED HAM

It's always Robert's job to prepare the ham at Christmas, and this is his recipe. He maintains that the rich Old Growler and a spot of whisky gives a wonderful flavour

½ Gammon
2 whole cloves
4 black peppercorns
1 tsp brown sugar

Topping:
25g (1oz) butter
50g (2oz) brown sugar
Pinch of ground cinnamon
1 tbsp whisky
150ml (¼pt) Nethergate Old
 Growler beer

Wash the gammon well under cold running water. Place into a large saucepan and barely cover with cold water, adding the cloves, peppercorns and sugar. Bring to the boil, remove any scum and then reduce to a simmer. Cover and cook for 1½hrs. Remove the gammon, cool slightly, but do not let it get cold, and peel off the skin. To make the topping, mix the butter, brown sugar, cinnamon and whisky together well. Score the top of the gammon fat with a diamond pattern and press the topping on to it firmly. Lift in to an ovenproof dish and pour the Old Growler around it. Bake in a preheated oven 190C, 375F or Gas Mark 5 for 30 minutes or until the topping is crisp and golden. Serve hot or cold.

RHUBARB CRISP

This pudding recipe is one handed down to Sally from Granny Bendall. Sally's two daughters love to make this pudding, which is quick and easy, and soon demolished by the family!

225g (8oz) rhubarb, chopped into
 2.5cm (1 inch) pieces
225g (8oz) bread, chopped into
 2.5cm (1 inch) cubes
175g (6oz) melted butter
110g (4oz) sugar
2 tbsps water

Grease an ovenproof dish. Put rhubarb in saucepan with a little water and about 2 tbps sugar, and gently simmer until softened. Transfer to ovenproof dish and put the bread cubes on top. Melt butter and sugar and then drizzle over the bread cubes. Bake in a preheated oven 180C, 350F, Gas Mark 4 for about 35–40 minutes until the topping is crisp and golden.

CHILLED LEMON FLAN

Whenever Sally needs to make something a bit special and impressive she makes this lemon flan, and says it's always a winner with guests.

Serves 4

For the base:
110g (4oz) digestive biscuits
50g (2oz) butter
1 level tbsp caster sugar

For the filling:
150ml (¼ pint) double cream
175g (6oz) can condensed milk
2 large lemons

For the topping:
Lightly whipped cream
Fresh or crystallised lemon slices

Crush digestive biscuits with a rolling pin. Melt butter in a pan, add sugar then blend in biscuit crumble. Mix well. Turn mixture into a 18cm (7 inch) pie plate or flan dish and press into shape round base and sides of plate with the back of a spoon. Bake in a slow oven (140C, 275F, Gas Mark 1) for 8 minutes. Remove from the oven and leave to cool. Do not turn the flan case out of dish as it will crumble.

Mix together cream, condensed milk and finely grated lemon rind. Slowly beat in lemon juice. Pour mixture into the flan case and chill for several hours until firm. Just before serving decorate the flan with a whirl of lightly whipped cream and the lemon slices.

Nellie Smith

When my Lavenham Church Cookbook was published last year, many people in the village asked me why Nellie Smith hadn't appeared in the book; well that was easily solved. Relatively new to Lavenham, I didn't know Nellie. This was soon rectified, and I have now met her many times.

Nellie is ninety-three years of age, and as bright as a button, with a mind to match. I am always amazed at her fund of knowledge; she can remember events and dates that have taken place in the early 20th century, and was one of the easiest subjects I had to interview, she is a good talker, and was always quick to correct me if I got a date or place wrong – for a ninety-three year old she is amazing.

But Nellie's life has been hard at times, and many sacrifices made to return to the family home and look after her parents. Nellie has no regrets, and her story is one that many older folk will be able to identify with. It began long before the television and computer technology age came on the scene, and all the other things we now take for granted, but it's also one of contentment and serenity, of learning too, although Nellie left school as soon as she was old enough. Writing this profile of her I feel I am not doing her full justice, but let's look at it as 'a preview in advance of a bigger release'! This is Nellie's story.

"I was born in Dovercourt in 1906 and left school at the age of 14. At that time there was very little opportunity for work in Dovercourt, and I was 17 when I started my first job as a nursemaid, looking after the vicar's youngest child, for the princely sum of five shillings (50p) a week. I was terrified of the vicar's wife, who treated me unkindly, and when I reached the age of 18 I left her employment. I went to London and soon got a job working as a house-maid for a family in Cumberland Terrace. I settled down and was very happy, and I stayed with this family for nearly two years. Then I was needed at home, my mother had been taken ill and I had to return to Dovercourt to nurse her. In those days it was called 'duty', and you did it gladly and without question, not giving a thought to your own ambitions or desires.

"After a while I managed to get work on a remote farm in the village of Oakley, just outside Dovercourt. The work was hard, and the hours long, and I had to sleep under the eaves in a tiny attic, which was cold and bare. I didn't stay long on this farm, and after three weeks I ran away and went back to my home in Dovercourt, and got a job locally as a house parlour maid, working for an old lady. The house was a large Victorian one with 12 rooms and overlooked the seafront. Besides me there was a cook and an 'old boy' who used to come and look after the lawns, and do any odd jobs around the house and garden. I stayed in this job for six years, but by then I was beginning to feel a bit more independent and wanted to spread my wings a bit………

"I had heard that jobs were being offered in the Military Hospital in Colchester, and I applied for one. Much to my surprise I was accepted, and I began working as a maid in the dining room of the Nursing Sisters' quarters. This was fine for a while, but I decided to try my luck in London again.

"After going for several interviews, I was taken on by a General, recently retired from the Indian Army, as his house parlour maid, and I remember this as being one of my happiest working periods. I used to have a reasonable amount of time off, and enjoyed going for walks and exploring the area around Campden Hill Square, where the General and his family lived. There was a library nearby, and I was able to read many books, something there hadn't been much time for in the past. One morning the General called me into his study and told me that the lease on the Campden Hill house had run out, and said he had decided to return to India, taking his family with him.

"Well, that was an unexpected blow, and after four and a half years working for the General and his family, I was once more without a job, but luck was on my side, and I soon found another job working for a family in one of the Grace and Favour houses in Gordon Place, Kensington. The family, a photographer and his teacher wife, had no need of a house parlour maid, but wanted a cook-housekeeper. They decided to give me a trial period, and I suppose you could say this was the start of my cooking career. I stayed with this family right up until the war broke out, and then they moved away from London and went to live in the country, leaving me behind.

"My family had now moved to Lavenham, and I had no choice but to return home again. I began working as a cook-housekeeper at the Lavenham Hall where I stayed for 18 months. I then joined the WAAFS, and rose to the rank of a Leading Aircraft Woman. This was a completely different life for me, and I thoroughly enjoyed the comradeship of my companions in the forces. After serving two years in the forces my mother died and I was again called home, this time to look after my father – a 'compassionate discharge' I believe they called it. I worked in a variety of jobs when I returned to Lavenham. I was employed by a market gardening company for a short while, and with the local stock horse factory; and for six years I worked in the Wool Hall, which belonged to the Railway Company. It was used as a convalescent home for railway staff and their families, until Mr. Beeching closed some of the railways down in the 1960s.

"By now my father had died, and I was able to return to cooking again. Reginald Brill, the well-known English realist painter had recently been appointed Warden of the Little Hall in Lavenham, and I was offered the job of cooking for Mr. and Mrs. Brill, and acting as their housekeeper. Mr. Brill used to have art students staying at Little Hall, so I had about six art students to cook for as well. This was another happy period in my working life, and I stayed with Mr. and Mrs. Brill for 12 years, until Mr. Brill died in 1974. Casting my mind back, I remember how tired he looked on the evening of 13 June, and I was so sad to learn the next morning that he had died of a heart attack. He was a lovely man to work for, and had the quirky habit of drawing little pictures on my pay packet, and I quite looked forward to seeing what he had drawn each week. These pictures have since been reproduced in a book called 'Reginald Brill', written by Judith Bumpus.

"Well I was now sixty-two years of age, but retirement was far from my mind, and I wanted to carry on working. At that time, the Angel Hotel in Lavenham needed a cook so I applied for the job, and was taken on by a Mr. and Mrs. Cheshire. In fact I worked for three licensees during the 28 years I was there – Mr. and Mrs. Graves, and the joint licensees, Mr. and Mrs. Whitcombe and Mr. and Mrs. Barry who are still there. Then I had a nasty fall, breaking my wrist, so I was forced to give up work, and that put an end to my cooking career! But I still keep busy, baking cakes for friends, the Hospice and local bazaars."

At 93 years of age Nellie is still agile and active. She does the crossword each day in her daily newspaper, loves to cook still, and keeps her tiny bungalow spotless. The fruit cakes she bakes, studded with jewels of fruit and nuts are always a sell-out at local bazaars and fayres in Lavenham. So far I haven't been able to prize the recipe from her, but here are three of her well tried and tested ones, easy to make and all freeze well too.

MEAT BALLS IN TOMATO SAUCE

Serves 4

225g (8oz) lean minced beef
225g (8oz) pork sausage meat
50g (2oz) breadcrumbs
1 egg
1 finely chopped onion
1 tbsp oil
A little butter
Salt and pepper
1 tsp paprika

Sauce:
200ml (7floz) beef stock
400g (14oz) can tomatoes, sieved
   with their juice
Pinch of sugar
½ tsp dried thyme
1 tbsp flour

Put the mince, sausage meat, onion, bread and paprika into a bowl with the beaten egg. Mix well and, with floured hands, form into 8 balls. Heat the oil and a little butter in a pan and fry until browned all over. Blend 10g (½oz) butter and the flour in a saucepan, and then add the stock. Heat, whisking continuously until it boils and thickens, and is smooth. Add the tomatoes, sugar and thyme. Season to taste, cover and simmer for 30 mins. Place the meatballs in a single layer in a shallow ovenproof serving dish. Cover with sauce and bake at 180C, 350F, Gas Mark 4 for about 30 mins. Serve with freshly cooked spaghetti.

APRICOT TART

Serves 6

One 23cm (9 inch) short crust flan
   case, pre-cooked blind

75g (3oz) butter
75g (3oz) caster sugar
Grated rind of one orange
2 eggs, beaten
110g (4oz) ground almonds
¼ tsp almond essence
2 tbsp orange juice
400g (14oz) can apricot halves,
   drained

Hot sieved apricot jam

Beat all the ingredients together, except the orange peel and apricot halves. Stir the orange peel into the mixture, and spread into the pastry case. Press apricots on top, rounded side up and bake in preheated oven 180C, 350F, Gas Mark 4 until set and golden brown. Brush over with hot jam to glaze. Can be eaten warm or cold.

CHERRY AND PRESERVED GINGER CAKE

175g (6oz) soft margarine or butter
175g (6oz) caster sugar
110g (4oz) self-raising flour
75g (3oz) plain flour
50g (2oz) ground almonds
3 eggs
110g (4oz) cherries, washed, dried
  and halved
110g (4oz) preserved ginger,
  chopped

Grease and line a 12cm (7 inch) cake tin or a 1lb loaf tin. Pre-heat oven to 180C, 350F, Gas Mark 4.

Cream sugar and butter until white and fluffy. Beat in the eggs with a spoonful of flour to prevent curdling. Sieve the two flours together and fold into the eggs, sugar and butter. Add the ground almonds and, lastly, stir in the cherries and ginger. If necessary, add a little milk to make a soft dropping consistency. Turn into the prepared tin, dust with a little caster sugar, and bake in preheated oven 180C, 350F, Gas Mark 4. for 1¼hrs, until golden brown.

Richard Evans

I first met Richard Evans a few years ago at a local Farmers' Market. He had a very small stall, and at that time was nowhere near as organised as he is today. Sometimes I seemed to be his only customer so he had time to chat to me, and told me how he had always had a long time interest in organic farming, that his ambition had been to work on an organic farm when he left school, had tried to find a job on one, but had not been successful; instead Richard went to work for Richard Seabrook, a sheep farmer near Bury, where he learnt all about sheep farming. This led to him setting up as a shearing contractor, and eventually, through his contract sheep work, finding a derelict farm to rent.

As happens in life Richard had a series of lucky breaks, which enabled him to buy Stonehouse Farm, and marry his former employer's daughter, Sue Seabrook. With the purchase of Stonehouse Farm, and renting some land he now markets his own beef and lamb. He is now also gradually building up a strong customer base, and supplies prepacked frozen meat to mail order customers, as well as supplying his regular ones, and selling his meat at local Farmers' Markets in the area. His hardwork and determination has now been rewarded, and his farm has been certified as being completely organic by the Soil Association.

Sue and Richard now have four small children, and although Sue helps as much as she can, the farm is not profitable enough to support the whole family, so Richard does other farming work to help cover costs and feed his young family. From what I have seen of Richard and Sue's enthusiasm for organic farming I am sure that the combination of organic conversion, and selling by direct marketing good quality meat, will help to redress the balance, which will eventually put their British beef and lamb well and truly on the map.

Sue has a busy lifestyle and most of her cooking tends to be on the simple side. She likes her cooking to rely on the traditional flavours of meat and vegetables, and adds very little in the way of flavours or herbs. Most of her vegetables are steamed, so that none of the true flavours are lost, serving them with a little butter.

Sue's steak and kidney pudding, and "any old fruit upside-down pudding" are two family favourites, and are quick and easy to follow. The sponge mixture in the pudding can also be used to make small buns, just add some fruit or fruit juice to give extra flavour, or you can add sultanas and a mashed banana, children love this combination.

STEAK AND KIDNEY PUDDING

2 lambs kidneys, skinned, cored
   and cut into small pieces
450-500g (1lb–1½lb) stewing or
   rump steak, cut into chunks
1 onion, chopped
250ml (9floz) beef stock
Salt and pepper
4 tbsp plain flour
Knob of butter or tbsp oil
110g (4oz) self-raising flour
50g (2oz) wholemeal flour
1 tsp baking powder
75g (3oz) suet
1 egg, beaten
A little water
Fresh herbs, when available –
   parsley

Toss steak and kidney in seasoned flour and fry in butter or oil until well browned on the outside, and soften onions in pan with the meat, then add stock and place in a casserole dish. Cook in a slow oven 150C, 300F, Gas Mark 2 for 1½ hours, and set aside until required.

Mix all dry ingredients together, including the herbs. Add beaten egg and enough cold water to make a soft dough, and set aside in fridge until required. 10–15 mins. before serving time line large greased pudding basin with dough, trimming around top edge. Fill basin with steak and kidney mixture and seal top with rolled out trimmings of dough. Cover and seal with cling film and cook in microwave on high for 8–10 mins.

BEEF IN BEER

Last winter this recipe appeared on Richard's stall at one of the Farmers' Markets in Needham Market. At the side of the stall there was also a casserole of "Beef in Beer" bubbling away on a burner for customers to try and I didn't need any coaxing – it was delicious, and very welcome on that bitterly cold day in February.

1.4kg (3lb) stewing beef, cubed
75g (3oz) butter
3 onions, sliced
4 cloves garlic, crushed and
   chopped
Salt and black pepper
1 level tbsp plain flour
300ml (½ pint) beef or vegetable
   stock (cube)
425ml (¾ pint) strong beer
1 tbsp wine vinegar
2 bay leaves

Melt the butter in a large casserole and add the cubed beef. Sauté until brown, drain and transfer to plate. Cook the sliced onion until trans-parent and add the garlic. Remove from pan. Scrape the juices together, stir in the flour and make a roux. Gradually add the beer and stock to make the sauce. Finally add the vinegar, bay leaves, salt and pepper. Put the meat and onion mixture carefully back into the casserole dish and cover. Cook in preheated oven 150C, 300F, Gas Mark 3 for about 2 hours. This casserole can be cooked ahead of time, and improves in flavour if reheated. You can also make it special by topping it with garlic bread and crisping it in the oven.

ANY 'OLD' FRUIT UPSIDE-DOWN PUDDING

This recipe is based on a Victoria Sponge mixture.

110g (4oz) soft margarine
110g (4oz) caster sugar
110g (4oz) self-raising flour
Pinch salt
1 tsp cornflour
2 large beaten eggs
Knob of butter and a little sugar

Beat all the above ingredients together to a smooth mixture. Melt sugar and butter in small flat dish and arrange fruit, with a little fruit juice in dish. Pour sponge mixture on top and bake in moderate oven 180C, 350F, Gas Mark 4 for 30–40 mins. When mixing sponge mixture you can add a little of the syrup or juice to the flavour it.

Christmas pudding

Apple turnover and éclairs

Fruit cake

Fruit loaf, breads and rolls

Stuffed pork joint

My very light scones

Victoria sponge

Cherry fruit cake

Afternoon tea, rock cakes, fancies and carrot cake

PART TWO

My Kind of Cooking

No introduction is necessary for the second part of my book, as the pages will speak for themselves. Here you will find recipes I have collected over the years, some have been handed down from my mother, and many come from friends and relatives. I've tried to include many traditional ones, which you will probably recognise, or may have forgotten, but you'll find, with a little extra ingredient here and there, and by adding a sprinkling of your favourite herb or spice, will transform an every day dish into something quite different.

Bon appetit!

Pork pie

Soups, Starters, Savouries and Pasta

Curried Parsnip Soup 71

Italian Bean Soup 71

Cream of Carrot Soup 71

Lettuce and Tarragon Soup 72

Cream of Avocado Soup 72

Carrot and Potato Soup 73

Beetroot Soup 73

Green Pepper and Tomato Soup ... 73

Tangy Tuna Cocktail 74

Asparagus with Lemon Vinaigrette ... 74

Cheddar Cheese Creams 74

Pastry Topped Mushroom Pots ... 75

Chicken Liver Pate 75

Cucumber and Cheese Mousse ... 76

Gruyere Roulade 76

Stilton Pears 77

Stuffed Mushrooms 77

Celery Hearts and Cheese 77

Savoury Semolina Cheese 78

Herby Omelette 78

Tuna and Pasta Bake 78

Macaroni Cheese 79

Savoury Potato Wedges 79

Stuffed Tomatoes 79

Onion Savoury 80

Picnic Pasties 80

Cheese Souffle 80

Asparagus Eggs 81

Mushrooms au Gratin 81

Curried Chicken Tartlets 81

Egg Tartlets 82

Spinach and Bacon with Pasta ... 82

Spaghetti with Ham and
Mushroom Sauce 82

Basil and Garlic Sauce (Pesto)
for Pasta 83

Tomato Sauce 83

CURRIED PARSNIP SOUP

Serves 6–8

700g (1½lb) parsnips, chopped
1 medium onion, chopped
1 clove garlic
1½ litres (2pts) chicken stock or
  stock cubes and water
1–2 tsp curry powder
50g (2oz) butter
½ tsp cinnamon
½ tsp ground cumin
150ml (5floz) single cream
Seasoning to taste
Chives to garnish

Melt butter in large saucepan, then add garlic, onions and parsnips. Cover and cook for 10 minutes. Sweat, but do not brown. Add curry powder, cinnamon, cumin and seasoning. Stir well and cook for 3 minutes. Add stock and simmer for 45 minutes. Adjust seasoning if necessary. Liquidise mixture. Add cream and decorate with chives. **Can be frozen.**

ITALIAN BEAN SOUP

A good filling soup for winter days.
Serves 6

50g (2oz) red kidney beans or
  haricot beans
2 leeks
2 rashers bacon, chopped
225g (8oz) tomatoes (or 420g tin
  of tomatoes)
1 large carrot, turnip and onion,
  chopped
Seasoning
Bay leaf
1 medium sized packet of frozen
  peas
850ml (1½pts) stock of your
  choice, I usually use chicken
  stock cube

Cover beans with pint of cold water and leave overnight. Drain next day. Chop bacon. Slice leeks and skin tomatoes (if fresh ones). Fry bacon, carrot, turnip and onion in a little oil for about 10 minutes. Transfer to large saucepan and add leeks, tomatoes and 850ml (1½pts) stock. Add bay leaf, seasoning and drained beans. Cover and simmer until tender. Add frozen peas for the last ten minutes of cooking. Delicious served with warm crusty bread.

CREAM OF CARROT SOUP

A light creamy colourful soup.
Serves 4–6

450g (1lb) carrots
225g (8oz) tomatoes
850ml (1½pts) chicken stock
300ml (½pt) milk
75g (3oz) butter
Chopped parsley, pepper and salt

Slice carrots thinly. Peel and chop tomatoes. Melt butter in thick saucepan and cook carrots for 3 minutes. Add tomatoes and cook for another 3 minutes. Pour in the stock and season. Simmer till carrots are soft. Put in blender. Return to pan and add hot milk. Garnish with parsley. A light creamy colourful soup.

LETTUCE AND TARRAGON SOUP

Involves quite a bit of time and effort, but you will be rewarded by the taste and presentation.

1 good head of lettuce
1 small onion
25g (1oz) butter
½ tsp dried tarragon
1 tbsp flour
1½ litres (2pts) chicken stock
½ cucumber
2 egg yolks
150ml (¼ pint) double cream
Salt, pepper, nutmeg, and fried
  croutons

Cut the washed and dried lettuce into ribbons and finely chop the onion. Melt the butter over a gentle heat and sweat the onion until it is transparent. Stir in the lettuce and tarragon, and continue to cook gently for another 5 minutes until the lettuce is soft. Take off the heat and stir in flour, return pan to stove and gradually add half the stock, a little at a time, blending it in. Simmer for 25 minutes. Whilst this is cooking, peel and deseed the half cucumber, then cut it into fine matchsticks. Allow soup to cool a little before pureeing it in the liquidiser or rubbing it through a fine sieve. Return it to the pan and add the rest of the stock. Beat together the egg yolks and cream, then stir into them some of the warm soup – to prevent any curdling – and blend this back into the soup. Season well. Add the julienne of cucumber and reheat the soup, but do not allow it to boil. Serve the soup with croutons fried in butter.

CREAM OF AVOCADO SOUP

Serves 4–6

40g (1½oz) butter
110g (4oz) onion, peeled and
  chopped
1 large avocado
1 tbsp flour
600ml (1pt) chicken stock cube
150ml (¼pt) creamy milk
Sea salt and pepper
Lemon slices

Melt butter in saucepan, add onion and sauté until tender, but not coloured.

Halve the avocado along the length, twist halves to separate and remove stone. Peel away the skin, roughly dice flesh, and toss the avocado in lemon juice. Add flour to onion, cook a little longer then add stock and avocado. Simmer covered for 10–15 mins. Remove from heat, add milk and season well. Puree in blender, or put through a sieve. Serve hot with croutons, garnish with wafer thin slices of lemon.

CARROT AND POTATO SOUP

Serves 6–8

1kg (2¼lb) carrots, peeled and
  diced
450g (1lb) potatoes, peeled and
  sliced
1 onion, peeled and chopped
1 stick celery, cleaned and sliced
50g (1oz) butter
600ml (1 pint) vegetable stock
  (cube can be used)
600ml (1 pint) milk
Salt and pepper to taste

1 tbsp parsley, chopped

Melt butter in large saucepan and
cook prepared vegetables. When
soft, add stock and seasoning.
Cover pan and simmer for about
1 hour. Then liquidize and return to
saucepan. Thin down puree as
desired with milk and reheat. Serve
garnished with parsley.

BEETROOT SOUP

This soup is delicious, and looks good too – you can serve it hot or cold.
Serves 4–6

225g (½lb) potatoes, peeled and
  chopped
225g (½lb) onions, peeled and
  chopped
225g (½lb) beetroots, peeled and
  sliced
25g (1oz) butter
900ml (1½pts) stock (you can use
  chicken stock cube)
50ml (2floz) double cream
Half a wine glass of sherry
Salt and pepper

Melt butter in a large saucepan and

cook the chopped onions and
potatoes on a low heat with the lid
on for about 10 minutes. Then add
the sliced beetroot and continue
cooking until the vegetables are
soft and the butter is absorbed.
Make sure you do not let the
vegetables brown. Add stock and
season to taste, bring to the boil
and simmer for about 1 hour.
Liquidize the soup, return to the
pan and reheat and add the sherry,
and at the last minute stir in the
cream.

GREEN PEPPER AND TOMATO SOUP

Serves 4

450g (1lb) tomatoes, skinned and
  sliced
2 medium green peppers, sliced
1 large onion, peeled and sliced
10g (1oz) butter
1 tbsp plain flour
900ml (1½ pints) chicken stock
4 tbsp cream
Salt and pepper to taste

Melt butter in a large saucepan.
Add the sliced vegetables and
sauté for 5 minutes. Stir in the
flour, gradually adding the stock.
Bring to the boil and simmer for
20 minutes. Then liquidize. Season
to taste, and swirl cream on top of
soup just before serving.

TANGY TUNA COCKTAIL

This tasty starter can also be served as a lunch for two with hot garlic bread.

Serves 4

200g (7oz) can tuna, drained
2 hard boiled eggs, chopped
8–10 radishes, sliced
2 large or 4–6 small gherkins,
  thinly sliced
Crisp lettuce leaves, to serve
Chopped parsley and lemon
  wedges to garnish

Dressing:
1 tsp Dijon mustard
2 tsp each lemon juice and white
  wine vinegar
Salt and pinch cayenne pepper
2 tbsp salad oil

Flake the tuna and mix with the eggs, radishes and gherkins. Make the dressing: beat the mustard, lemon juice, vinegar, salt and pepper together in a small bowl. Whisk in the salad oil gradually to blend. Pour dressing over tuna mixture and toss lightly. Chill for up to 2hrs. Spoon the tuna on to lettuce leaves and serve garnished with chopped parsley and the lemon wedges. Good served with sliced pumpernickel or rye bread and butter, or hot garlic or herb bread.

ASPARAGUS WITH LEMON VINAIGRETTE

Serves 4

700g (1½lb) fresh asparagus
Thin strips of lemon rind
Lemon vinaigrette
2–3 tbsp lemon juice
6 tbsp sunflower oil
1 tsp caster sugar
1 tsp French mustard
Salt and pepper to taste
Pinch of red pepper flakes

Cut off tough ends of asparagus. Cook spears in boiling, salted water for 8–12 minutes, depending on thickness, until just tender. Drain and rinse under cold running water to prevent further cooking and help retain colour. Drain well. Arrange in bundles on serving dish and 'tie' with strips of lemon rind. Whisk vinaigrette ingredients together and pour into a jug. Serve at once with the asparagus or chill both until required.

CHEDDAR CHEESE CREAMS

Serves 6

6 rashers streaky bacon
175g (6oz) Cheddar cheese
300ml (½pt) whipping cream
2 eggs
Salt and cayenne pepper

Grill bacon until crisp enough to break into small pieces. Crumble into 6 ramekin dishes. Sprinkle cheese evenly between each dish. Whisk eggs into cream with salt and cayenne pepper to taste, and pour into ramekins. Cook in preheated oven 200C, 400F, Gas Mark 6 for about 15 minutes. Serve immediately

PASTRY TOPPED MUSHROOM POTS

Deliciously aromatic creamed mushrooms, hidden under a topping of crisp pastry. Be sure to use ovenproof soup bowls.

Serves 4

1 medium onion, chopped
2 tbsp chopped fresh parsley
25g (1oz) butter
4tsp plain flour
600ml (1pt) chicken stock cube
450g (1lb) open mushrooms, trimmed and sliced
250ml (8floz) single cream
1 tbsp Worcestershire sauce
Salt and pepper to taste
300g (11oz) frozen puff pastry, thawed
1 egg, beaten

Fry onion and parsley gently in butter. Stir in flour and cook for 2 mins. Gradually stir in stock to make a smooth sauce. Bring to the boil, then add mushrooms and cream and simmer for 10 mins. Season with Worcestershire sauce, salt and pepper. Remove from heat and allow to cool. Heat oven to 220C, 425F, Gas Mark 7. Roll out pastry and cut into circles about 2.5cm (1 inch) larger than bowls. Fill bowls with mixture. Brush rims with beaten egg and cover with pastry, pressing the edges to the bowls. Decorate with pastry, brush with egg and bake for 10–15 mins. until well risen and golden.

CHICKEN LIVER PATE

This recipes makes approximately 350g (¾lb).

Serves 4–6

600ml (1pt) water
2 tsp salt
½ tsp celery salt
2 sprigs parsley
4 peppercorns
225g (8oz) chicken livers
¼ tsp Tabasco sauce
110g (4oz) butter
Pinch grated nutmeg and 1 tsp dry mustard
Pinch ground cloves
1 clove garlic
1 small onion, finely chopped, gently cooked with little butter
1 tbsp brandy or dry sherry
25g (1oz) stuffed green olives for decoration

In a large saucepan bring the water to the boil. When boiling add pinch of salt, celery salt, parsley and peppercorns. Reduce heat to moderate and simmer for 10 minutes. Add chicken livers, cover pan and cook for a further 10 minutes. Drain livers through strainer and liquidise. Add all remaining ingredients and blend thoroughly. Put pate into 600ml (1pt) terrine or dish, smooth top and decorate with sliced olives. Place in fridge and chill for at least 6 hours. Serve with slices of brown toast or slices of French crusty bread.

CUCUMBER AND CHEESE MOUSSE

Serves 4–6

1 large cucumber
175g (6oz) curd or cream cheese
1 tsp onion juice
Salt and white pepper
150ml (¼pt) boiling water or
    vegetable stock
10g (½oz) gelatine, soaked in 3
    tbsp cold water
1 tbsp white wine vinegar
1 tbsp caster sugar
Pinch ground mace
350g (¾pt) double cream, lightly
    whipped

Dice the cucumber very finely, sprinkle with salt and leave it pressed between two plates for 30 minutes. Work the cheese with onion juice and seasoning. Pour boiling water or stock on to gelatine, stir until it is dissolved, then add it to cheese. Drain the diced cucumber thoroughly and mix it with vinegar, sugar and spice. When the cheese mixture is quite cold, fold in the cucumber and the cream. Pour into the prepared mould and leave to set.

GRUYERE ROULADE

175g (6oz) Gruyere cheese, grated
2 tbsp grated Parmesan cheese
50g (2oz) fresh breadcrumbs
150ml (¼pt) double cream
4 eggs, separated
Pinch cayenne pepper
Salt

Line a 25 x 30cm (10" x 12") Swiss roll tin with oiled and non-stick paper and sprinkle with 1 tbsp of Parmesan cheese. Mix the bread-crumbs, Gruyere cheese, cream, egg yolks, cayenne pepper and salt. Whisk egg whites until they form soft peaks and fold into cheese mixture. Spread evenly in the prepared tin and bake in a preheated oven 190C, 375F, for 10 minutes until firm to the touch. Leave to cool, then turn out onto a clean towel sprinkled with Parmesan cheese.

Filling:
Scrambled eggs and cream cheese, or for a special dinner party, thinly sliced slices of smoked salmon mixed with lemon juice and freshly ground black pepper, makes a luxurious alternative.

Mix ingredients together gently, spread the filling right to the edges of the roulade and roll up, and don't worry if some cracks appear, it just makes the roulade look more interesting!

STILTON PEARS

An unusual starter made with dessert pears filled with a savoury cheese stuffing. Peach halves make a good alternative to pears, and go well with Gorgonzola cheese and almonds.

Serves 4

2 x 411g (14½oz) cans of pear
   halves in natural juice, drained
175g (6oz) Stilton cheese,
   crumbled
50g (2oz) cream cheese
1 tbsp Port, optional
Black pepper, to taste
Chopped walnuts, to garnish
Salad leaves to serve

Select 8 pear halves and place cut side uppermost on a plate. Trim base to level, if necessary. Place remaining pears and trimmings in a food processor or blender with Stilton and blend until smooth. Blend in cream cheese, port and pepper. Spoon or pipe cheese mixture into centre of each pear half. Sprinkle with nuts. Serve lightly chilled on a bed of salad leaves.

STUFFED MUSHROOMS

Serves 6

1 dsp butter
1 dsp chopped ham
1 tbsp chopped parsley and
   shallot
Grated lemon rind
1 dsp fine breadcrumbs
A little stock
½ dozen large mushrooms
Salt and pepper
Some sprigs of parsley

Melt butter in saucepan and stir in chopped ham and parsley, and then add remaining ingredients except mushrooms. Simmer for 5 minutes. Prepare mushrooms by peeling, washing, drying and removing stalks. Arrange with stalk side up on a greased baking dish and put a little mixture on each. Cover with greased paper and bake in hot oven 200C, 400F, Gas Mark 6 for about 20 minutes. When cooked place each mushroom on a round of buttered toast and garnish with sprigs of parsley.

CELERY HEARTS AND CHEESE

This is one of the easiest of dishes to make, and can be eaten as a supper savoury or light luncheon meal.

Serves 4

1 large tin celery hearts
600ml (1pt) creamy cheese sauce
6 hard boiled eggs, halved
Little grated cheese

Put celery hearts and eggs in an ovenproof dish and cover with cheese sauce. Sprinkle with grated cheese and bake in preheated oven 180C, 350F, Gas Mark 4 for about 25–30 minutes, until golden brown and bubbly on top.

SAVOURY SEMOLINA CHEESE

This dish is a great favourite with all who have tasted it, and is quick and easy to prepare.

Serves 4

3 tbsp semolina
300ml (½pt) water
2 eggs
110g (4oz) cheese, grated
25g (1oz) butter
1 small onion
½ tsp salt – dash of pepper
½ tsp mixed herbs

Boil semolina in water with chopped onion, herbs and seasoning. When cooked add grated cheese and yolks of eggs. Leave to cool. At last minute beat whites of eggs until stiff, fold into mixture and put in hot dish which has been brushed with melted fat. Bake in preheated oven 180C, 350F, Gas Mark 4 for about ½ hour.

HERBY OMELETTE

Serves 2–3

1 medium onion
1 medium potato
6 tbsp olive oil
3 eggs and a pinch of salt
1 tsp mixed herbs

Peel and chop onion and fry in hot oil for 2–3 minutes. Peel potato and cut into small dice, add to the pan. Continue cooking until potato is tender and onion golden brown.

Beat the eggs with a pinch of salt and mixed herbs, and pour into pan. Stir ingredients lightly together with a fork, then leave to settle and cook gently until underside is golden brown. Carefully turn over by slipping omelette onto a plate, then turning it over into the pan to brown the other side. Serve immediately with thinly sliced fresh tomatoes.

TUNA AND PASTA BAKE

Serves 4

175g–200g (6–7oz) tin tuna flakes
    in brine
275g–300g (10–12oz) tin sweet
    corn
250g (9oz) pasta shells

Cheese Sauce:
10g (½oz) margarine
10g (½oz) corn flour
300ml (½pt) skimmed milk
50g (2oz) mild Cheddar cheese

Method to make sauce: Melt margarine, add corn flour, and mix to a paste. Then add skimmed milk gradually to achieve a light smooth sauce by constant stirring. Add grated cheese and stir until again smooth. Add sauce to cooked pasta. Place tuna in dish, then sweet corn and top with the pasta in sauce i.e. three complete layers of the ingredients.

MACARONI CHEESE

Serves 4

110g (4oz) whole-wheat macaroni
2 hard boiled eggs, chopped
2 fresh chopped tomatoes
425ml (¾pt) thick white sauce
175g (6oz) grated Cheddar cheese
10g (½oz) peas
35g (1½oz) sweet corn

Cook macaroni, peas and sweet corn. Make the white sauce and add 110g (4oz) of the grated cheese, then add macaroni, peas, sweet corn, chopped eggs and chopped tomatoes. Pour into casserole dish, sprinkle with the rest of the cheese on top with some slices of tomato. Cook in preheated oven 190C, 375F, Gas Mark 5 until the cheese has nicely browned on top.

SAVOURY POTATO WEDGES

Serves 4–6

700g (1½lb) cooked mashed
  potatoes
4 rashers of streaky bacon
225g (8oz) cooked chopped
  cabbage
2 skinned chopped tomatoes
50g (2oz) grated cheese
25g (1oz) butter
Salt and pepper

Cut up bacon and fry it in the butter until crisp. Strain the fat into a frying pan. Then mix together the bacon, potato, cabbage, tomatoes, cheese and seasoning. Reheat fat in pan, spread the potato mixture in the pan and cook over a medium heat until browned underneath. Upturn the pan over a large plate to tip out the potato cake, add a little more butter to pan and slide the cake back in to brown on the other side. Turn out on to a warm serving plate and cut into wedges. This makes a tasty supper dish, and adding a poached egg on each wedge, turns it into a light lunch.

STUFFED TOMATOES

4 large tomatoes
110g (4oz) cottage cheese
4 tsps chopped watercress leaves
4 level tsps mayonnaise
Salt and pepper

Stand the tomatoes on their stalk ends and cut a slice from the top of each one. Scoop out the seeds and flesh without breaking the skins. Chop the tomato flesh and mix with the cheese, watercress, mayonnaise and seasoning to taste. Pile the filling into the tomato shells, place the lids on top at an angle and serve with a green salad. Any savoury filling may be used for this recipe, and to serve hot, place on a lightly greased tin and bake at 190C, 375F, Gas Mark 5 for 20 minutes.

ONION SAVOURY

4 medium size onions
25g (1oz) butter
25g (1oz) plain flour
150ml (¼pt) onion stock
150ml (¼pt) milk
75g (3oz) grated Cheddar cheese
1 egg yolk

Cook onions in boiling salted water until tender, drain them (keeping back stock) and arrange in a fire-proof dish. Melt butter, add flour and cook, stirring in stock and milk. Stir vigorously over heat until the sauce is thick and smooth. Beat in the cheese, egg yolk and seasoning to taste, pour over the onions and place under the grill. When nicely browned serve garnished with triangles of toast

PICNIC PASTIES

These pasties are ideal to take on a picnic, and they taste just as good hot or cold.

175g (6oz) ready-made puff pastry
75g (3oz) Cheddar cheese, grated
1 medium onion
1 heaped tsp made mustard
Salt and pepper
Beaten egg

Divide the pastry into 4 and roll out into rounds. Grate the onion finely and mix with the cheese, bread-crumbs, mustard and seasoning. Place some of the mixture on each pastry round, damp the edges, and fold over one half to make a semi circle. Seal the edges well and brush over with egg. Bake at 220C, 425F, Gas Mark 7 for 20–25 minutes.

CHEESE SOUFFLE

I have made this Cheese Soufflé many times, and it has always turned out perfect, in fact it's guaranteed foolproof!
Serves 4

35g (1½oz) butter
4 egg yolks
5 egg whites
2 tbsps flour
225ml (8floz) boiling milk
75g (3oz) mature Cheddar cheese, grated
Pinch of nutmeg, cayenne and pepper
½ tsp salt

Melt butter over a low heat, stir in flour until the mixture foams, but do not let it brown. Remove from heat, when it stops foaming pour in all the boiling milk at once, stirring all the time. Beat egg yolks, one at a time, into the mixture. Beat 5 egg whites very stiffly with the salt, and stir about one-quarter of them into the yolk mixture, stir in the grated cheese and then very gently fold in the remaining whites. Turn mixture into a buttered 2½pt (1.5 litre) soufflé dish. Pre-heat oven to 200C, 400F, Gas mark 6, but as soon as soufflé is put into the oven reduce temperature to 190C, 375F, Gas Mark 5 and cook for 35 minutes. When cooked serve immediately, using a warm spoon.

ASPARAGUS EGGS

Serves 4

3 hard-boiled eggs
3 rashers of lean bacon
115g (4½oz) grated cheese
1 small tin asparagus tips
3 tbsps butter
3 tbsps flour

Slice the eggs. Dice and fry the bacon. Make a sauce with butter, flour and asparagus liquid made up to 600ml (1pt) with milk. (Set aside one tbsp grated cheese.) Add the remaining cheese and stir in the asparagus, eggs and bacon. Place in an oven-proof dish and sprinkle with the set aside tbsp of grated cheese, dot with butter. Place in a preheated oven 180C, 350F, Gas Mark 4, or under a hot grill, until bubbling and golden brown.

MUSHROOMS AU GRATIN

Serves 3–4

225g (8oz) mushrooms
1 sliced onion
2 tbsp sunflower oil
2 tbsp flour
225ml (8floz) mushroom stock, made from stems
50g (2oz) fresh breadcrumbs
¼ tsp black pepper
¼ tsp paprika
20g (¾oz) butter
½ tsp salt
Juice of 1 lemon

Fry onions in oil. Add the flour and brown. Then add the stock, pepper, paprika, butter, salt and lemon juice and cook until the sauce has thickened. Slice mushrooms into quarters and add them to the sauce. Put into a baking dish, sprinkle with breadcrumbs and bake in preheated oven 190C, 375F, Gas Mark 5, until nicely browned and crisp on top.

CURRIED CHICKEN TARTLETS

Makes 4 tartlets

175g (6oz) short crust pastry
110g (4oz) walnuts, roughly chopped
150ml (¼ pint) mayonnaise
Chopped fresh parsley
2 tsp curry powder
2 tbsp lemon juice
350g (12oz) cooked chicken meat, cut into chunks
Salt and pepper

Divide pastry dough into four. Roll out each piece and use to line four 11.5cm (4½ inch) tartlet cases. Bake blind in preheated oven 190C, 375F, Gas Mark 5 for 12–15 minutes and allow to cool. Stir curry powder, lemon juice, walnuts and chicken into the mayonnaise and season to taste with salt and pepper. Spoon into the tartlet cases and sprinkle with chopped parsley. These can be eaten heated up, or they are ideal to take on a picnic and eaten cold.

EGG TARTLETS

Makes 6 tartlets

225g (8oz) short crust pastry
1 large garlic clove, crushed
4 tbsp chopped fresh basil
300ml (½ pint) mayonnaise
4 chopped hard-boiled eggs

Roll out dough to 5mm (¼ inch) thick. Use 10cm (4 inch) cutter, cut dough into 6 circles. Line 15cm x 7.6cm (6" x 3") fluted tartlet tins with dough, trimming off any excess. Place on baking sheet and bake blind in preheated oven 190C, 375F, Gas Mark 5 for 15–20 minutes. Remove from tins and allow to cool. Mix mayonnaise, garlic and basil together. Divide chopped egg between the pastry cases and pour over enough of the mayonnaise mixture to fill the cases. Garnish each one with a slice of hard-boiled egg and a sprig of basil. Serve cold with salad.

SPINACH AND BACON WITH PASTA

Serves 4

25g (1oz) butter
1 onion, chopped
1 clove garlic, crushed
4 rashers bacon, chopped
2–3 bunches spinach, chopped
250g (9oz) pasta spirals, cooked

Melt butter in a large frying pan. Add onion, garlic and bacon. Cook until onion is lightly transparent and bacon is cooked. Stir in spinach and cook for a further 2 minutes or until spinach is a rich, dark green colour, stirring constantly. Pour over the hot pasta and serve.

SPAGHETTI WITH HAM AND MUSHROOM SAUCE

Serves 4–6

2 tbsp oil
2 ham steaks, chopped
1 onion, chopped
200g (7oz) mushrooms, sliced
250g (9oz) carton sour cream
1 egg yolk
Pepper
250g (9oz) spaghetti, cooked
1 tbsp chopped parsley

Heat oil in a frying pan or saucepan. Add ham and onion. Cook until onion is clear and ham slightly browned. Stir in mushrooms and cook for a further 2 minutes. Remove from heat. In a bowl beat sour cream and egg yolk together. Add this to ham mixture. Return pan to a low heat and cook, stirring constantly until sauce thickens slightly. Do not allow to boil. Season with pepper to taste. Add hot pasta, stir to combine and garnish with parsley.

BASIL AND GARLIC SAUCE (PESTO) FOR PASTA

Serves 4

200g (7oz) tagliatelle
1 tbsp oil
2 tbsp pine nuts
3 cloves garlic, chopped
50g (2oz) fresh basil leaves
4 tbsp olive oil
Salt and black pepper

Heat first measure of oil in a small frying pan. Add pine nuts and cook, stirring frequently until golden. Drain on absorbent paper. Put garlic, basil and pine nuts into a food processor or blender. Process until finely chopped. Continue processing while adding second measure of oil in a thin, steady stream. Process for a few seconds to just combine. Season with salt and pepper to taste. Serve over hot cooked pasta.

TOMATO SAUCE

Homemade tomato sauce wins hands down over the commercially bought version, and this sauce goes well over most pasta, with a little chopped parsley or basil to give extra flavour.

2 tbsp oil
1 onion, chopped
1 clove garlic, crushed
2 rashers bacon, chopped
1 stalk celery, chopped
1 tbsp plain flour
225ml (8floz) tomato puree
250ml (9floz) liquid beef stock (a stock cube will do)
½ tsp sugar
Salt and pepper

Heat oil in saucepan. Add onion, garlic, bacon and celery. Cook until golden. Stir in flour and cook until frothy. Mix in tomato puree. Remove from heat and cool slightly. Gradually add stock, stirring constantly. Add sugar. Return to heat and cook, stirring until mixture boils. Reduce heat and simmer gently for 45 minutes, or until sauce consistency is reached. Season with salt and pepper to taste. This amount of sauce will be sufficient for 250g (9oz) of hot pasta.

Main Courses

FISH

Fish Pie 87
Fish au Gratin 87
Mackerel With Lemon and
   Mustard 88
Crisp Herby Fish Cakes 88
Seafood Casserole 89
Savoury Baked Haddock 89
Salmon and Caper Flan 89
Seafood Risotto 90
Baked Trout 90
Salmon Filo Pie 91
Fish Chowder 91
Stuffed Herrings 92
Crab Morney Flan 92

MEAT
(beef, pork and lamb)

Paprika Goulash 93
Bacon and Onion Crumble 93
Pork Casserole 94
Herby Lamb Casserole 94
Parcel of Pork with Cider 94
Curried Veal 95
Beef and Cider Casserole 95
Herby Meat Balls 96
Beef Pot Roast 96
Chinese Style Roast Pork 97
Quick Raised Pork Pie 97
Cottage Pie with Leek and
   Potato Topping 98
Roast Lamb with Minty Stuffing
   Balls 98
Herby Faggots 99
Pork with Pineapple and Date
   Stuffing 99
Sausage and Bacon Risotto 100
Roast Liver 100

Beef Lentil Curry 100
Beef Loaf 101
Pork and Veal Plate Pie 101
Steak and Kidney Pie 102
Beef Steak and Mushroom
   Pudding 102
Stuffed Sausage Roll 103
Roast Stuffed Pork 103
Seville Pork 'Pot' 103

POULTRY AND GAME

Barbecued Chicken Casserole ... 104
Somerset Cider Chicken 104
Golden Crust Chicken Joints ... 105
Chicken and Broccoli Quiche ... 105
Cold Chicken Curry 105
Turkey with a Barbecue Sauce ... 106
Rich Chicken Pie 106
Turkey Burgers 107
Turkey Rolls 107
Roast Duck with Orange Sauce ... 108
Roast Apple Duckling 108
Pheasant Pie 109
Rabbit Pie 109
Venison Casserole 110

VEGETARIAN DISHES

Vegetarian Nut Roast 111
Nut Wellington 111
Cauliflower Surprise 112
Vegetable Hotpot 112
Marrow Bake 112
Vegetarian Lasagne 113
Vegetable Stroganoff 113
Stuffed Aubergines 114
Mushroom Tarts 114
Vegetable Burgers 115
Cheese and Celery Pie 115

FISH

FISH PIE

This recipes takes 1.5kg (2½lb) mixed fish after skinning and filleting.
Serves 8

450g (1lb) salmon, skinned and
  filleted
450g (1lb) haddock, skinned and
  filleted
225g (½lb) lemon sole, skinned
  and filleted
(You can use any firm white fish
  and add shell fish if you wish)
1 large onion, peeled and thinly
  sliced
700g (1½lb) mushrooms, thinly
  sliced
1kg (2¼lb) ripe tomatoes, peeled
  and sliced
175g–225g (6–8ozs) butter
300ml (½ pint) double cream
Chopped parsley
4 hard boiled eggs, roughly
  chopped (optional)
1kg (2¼lb) (approx) mashed
  potatoes

Cut fish into large cubes. Season with salt and pepper. Dip pieces in flour and fry in butter until lightly cooked, and set aside. Fry onion in butter until soft and golden. Add mushrooms and cook briefly. Add tomatoes. Cook all together for a few minutes. Season with salt and pepper. Mash potatoes with a little hot milk, butter, salt and pepper.

To assemble: Use a fairly deep 9cm to 10cm (3 to 4 inch) ovenproof dish. Place a layer of vegetables on the bottom. Sprinkle with chopped parsley and chopped egg. Follow with a layer of vegetables, parsley, egg; then fish, finishing with a layer of vegetables. Pour 300ml (½ pint) cream over the dish. Leave to soak in. Cover with the mashed potatoes. Decorate with a fork. Heat in preheated oven 180C, 350F, Gas Mark 4 for about 1¼ hours.

This dish may be completely assembled in advance. If necessary a day before. If this is done, make sure that all the ingredients are cold before assembling.

FISH AU GRATIN

Serves 2–3

225g (8oz) cooked fish (cold)
50g (2oz) butter
1 hard-boiled egg
50g (2oz) grated cheese
25g (1oz) bread crumbs
Pepper and salt

Flake fish and remove all bones and skin. Butter a pie dish, and put a layer of fish at the bottom, using about half of it. Chop the egg and distribute over the fish, put about 25g (1oz) of the butter over this (cut up in small pieces). Sprinkle a thin layer of grated cheese on top. Spread the remainder of the fish over the egg layer, sprinkle the remaining cheese over, then the bread crumbs, and lastly the remains of the butter in small pieces over the top. Bake in a preheated oven 180C, 350F, Gas Mark 4 for about 40 minutes, until it is crisp and golden on top.

MACKEREL WITH LEMON AND MUSTARD

Serves 4

4 shallots, finely chopped
110g (4oz) butter
175g (6oz) brown breadcrumbs
3 level tbsp whole mustard seeds
3 large lemons
4 egg yolks
4 mackerel
1 level tbsp mustard (English or
    French will do)
Fresh parsley to garnish

You will need the mackerel to be cleaned and boned, but left whole. Wash the fish thoroughly making sure the inside is clean. Place the four fish in a large, shallow, greased ovenproof dish, so that the fish sit evenly in it. Fry the onion in a little of the butter until soft and golden. Mix the breadcrumbs with the mustard seeds, grated rind of the lemons, mustard and egg yolks. Season to taste. Stuff this mixture into the cavity of the mackerel. Make deep cuts along the skin of the fish and dust them lightly with flour. Pour over the juice of the lemons and dot with the remaining butter. Cook, uncovered, in preheated oven 190C, 375F, Gas Mark 5 for about 35 minutes. Serve garnished with chopped parsley.

CRISP HERBY FISH CAKES

Serves 4

275g (10oz) cooked flaked white
    fish
275g (10oz) fresh boiled potatoes,
    mashed or put through strainer
25g (1oz) butter, melted
1 egg, beaten
1 tbsp finely chopped parsley
1 tbsp chives, chopped
1 tbsp Worcestershire sauce
1 egg, beaten and 110g (4oz) dried
    breadcrumbs (for frying)

Mix fish and potatoes in a warm bowl. Season well, add melted butter and mix well. Add beaten egg and chopped herbs, and chill for 30 minutes. Shape into eight flat cakes and coat in egg and bread crumbs. Fry in a hot shallow oil. Goes well with a hot spicy tomato sauce and sauté potatoes.

HOT SPICY TOMATO SAUCE
Place 700g (1½lb) roughly chopped tomatoes in a saucepan with 1 tbsp olive oil, 1 garlic clove, peeled and crushed. 1 tbsp fresh or dried basil, 1 tsp dry mustard. Bring to the boil and simmer for 15 minutes. Add chopped basil, pinch of chilli powder and sugar to taste, salt and pepper. Simmer for a further 5–10 minutes. Then pass through a sieve and reheat before serving.

SEAFOOD CASSEROLE

Serves 4

225g (8oz) prepared prawns
450g (1lb) filleted plaice, cut into
  small pieces
110g (4oz) mushrooms, sliced
425g (15oz) tin of drained asparagus
110g (4oz) almonds
600ml (1 pint) good white sauce (I
  make mine with cornflour, and
  add a wineglass of sherry)
50g (2oz) fresh white breadcrumbs
2 tbsp grated cheese

In a 900ml (1½ pint) deep casserole dish place alternate layers of prawns, mushrooms, almonds, fish pieces, asparagus. Season well. Pour white sauce round the edge of the fish in the dish and cover with crumbs and cheese. Bake in a preheated oven 180C, 350F, Gas Mark 4 for about 25 minutes. Remove lid and brown for another 10 minutes or so. This dish goes well with braised celery.

SAVOURY BAKED HADDOCK

This dish is quick and easy, and can be served for supper or a main meal with a jacket potato and salad.

Serves 4

4 medium sized fresh haddock fillets
4 tbsp dry sherry
Paprika
Grated Parmesan cheese
75g (3oz) cornflakes, finely crumbled
75g (3oz) butter
Salt and pepper

Butter a shallow ovenproof dish and put in the fillets, making sure to

remove any bones. Sprinkle with salt and pepper and pour over the sherry, making sure it goes under the fish. Dot half the butter, sprinkle liberally with paprika and cheese, and cover with a layer of cornflakes and the remaining butter. Cook in preheated oven at 220C, 425F, Gas Mark 7 for about 25–30 minutes until nicely crisp and lightly browned on top.

SALMON AND CAPER FLAN

Serves 4

225g (8oz) ready-made short crust
  pastry
2 tbsp olive oil
1 small can tinned salmon
1 dsp capers
3 large eggs, beaten
150ml (¼ pint) milk
150ml (¼ pint) double cream
1 medium can salmon
A little parsley, chopped
6 spring onions, finely chopped

Roll out pastry and use to line an 18cm (7 inch) deep-fluted loose

bottom quiche tin. Prick base and chill for 25 minutes. Heat oil and fry spring onions for 5 mins. Beat together eggs, cream and milk. Season to taste. Preheat oven to 200C, 400F, Gas Mark 6. Scatter onions over pastry base, spread the flaked salmon evenly on top, and sprinkle the capers over. Pour egg mixture carefully over the top and cook for approximately 45–50 minutes, until the quiche is risen and firm to the touch.

SEAFOOD RISOTTO

Another seafood dish, but one that is versatile – you can alter the fish ingredients according to your taste.

Serves 6

450g (1lb) long grained rice
1 small tin shrimps
1 small tin prawns
1 medium tin crabmeat
1 medium jar of cockles
4 or 5 scampi
1 medium onion, peeled and chopped
110g (4oz) mushrooms, sliced
1 small red pepper
Tomato ketchup
Cayenne pepper to taste
A little butter

Boil rice in salted water for about 20 minutes. Pour into a sieve and pour cold water through to separate the grains. Drain well and when dry transfer to fireproof oven dish. Strain off liquid from tins of fish, and add the fish to the rice, cutting up the crab and scampi into small pieces. Fry onion in butter until tender and golden, and add to the fish mixture. Then fry mushrooms and pepper separately in butter and add also to the fish mixture. Mix all together with enough tomato ketchup to colour and moisten. Season with cayenne pepper. Heat through slowly in a moderate oven with the lid on the dish. Serve with brown buttered toast.

BAKED TROUT

Serves 4

4 Trout, about 225g (8oz) each
75g (3oz) mushrooms, chopped
1 lemon
110g (4oz) breadcrumbs
50g (2oz) onion, finely chopped
1 tbsp parsley, chopped
Salt, pepper and butter

Melt onion gently in 50g (2oz) butter for about 10 minutes until it is golden. Mix with breadcrumbs, mushrooms and parsley. Season well with salt, pepper, lemon juice and zest.

Cut 4 pieces of foil approximately 30.5cm (12 inch) square. In the centre of each spread a generous dollop of butter along the 12.5cm (5 inch) line. Put stuffing on top of butter, dividing equally between the 4 bits of foil, then put the trout on top of the stuffing. Make foil into loose envelopes, twisting ends to seal. Bake in preheated oven at 170C, 325F, Gas Mark 3 for about 35 minutes.

This recipe came from The Leonard Cheshire Foundation book of Favourite Recipes, and was contributed by Lord and Lady Home.

SALMON FILO PIE

Serves 4

450g (1lb) salmon fillet, skinned
Juice of ½ a lemon
250g (9oz) can of asparagus
225g (8oz) cream cheese
1 tbsp parsley, chopped
A few sprigs of dill, roughly
    chopped
25g (1oz) butter, melted with 2
    tbsp oil
1 medium packet filo pastry
Seasoning

Trim salmon if necessary and slice across any thick parts of the fillet to make an even thickness. Sprinkle the salmon with salt, pepper and lemon juice. Drain the asparagus and place in a food processor with the dill, parsley, cream cheese, and seasoning. Blend until smooth. Grease a 23cm (9") loose bottomed cake tin or a fairly deep flan tin.

Brush a sheet of the filo pastry with the butter oil mixture and lay in the tin with the ends hanging over a little. Repeat this covering all over the tin, overlapping the pieces, and using all but 3 pieces of the pastry. Lay the salmon evenly in the base of the tin, covering the base, then top with the asparagus mixture. Fold the overlapping pastry in, cover the pie with two of the remaining sheets of filo. Cut the remaining pastry sheets into strips and roll up to make rosettes and brush all over the top with the oil mixture. Bake in preheated oven 180C, 350F, Gas Mark 4 for 40–50 minutes; if the top becomes too brown, reduce the heat a little, and cover top with a little foil. This pie can be eaten hot or cold, and may be frozen cooked or uncooked.

FISH CHOWDER

This is a substantial thick soup, with the vegetables making it enough for a main course.
Serves 6–8

1 medium sized onion, peeled and
    chopped
2 stalks celery, washed and diced
25g (1oz) butter
450g (1lb) potatoes, peeled and
    diced
2 medium sized carrots, washed,
    scraped and diced
600ml (1 pint) water
450g (1lb) fresh cod or haddock
300ml (½ pint) milk
Salt and freshly ground black
    pepper

Melt butter in large pan, then add onion and celery and cook gently for a few minutes. Add potatoes, carrots and water to pan and bring to the boil and simmer for 10–20 minutes until vegetables are tender. Skin fish and cut into 2.5cm (1 inch) cubes and add to pan. Simmer for another 10 minutes. Add milk and reheat gently. Season and serve.

STUFFED HERRINGS

4 fresh herrings with soft roes
Lemon slices and sprigs of parsley

For the stuffing:
Soft roes
1 tbsp chopped parsley
1 tbsp grated onion
1 clove garlic
4 rounded tbsp fresh white
  breadcrumbs
2 hard boiled eggs
A little milk
Salt and pepper

Clean the herrings, remove back bone and reserve roes (you can ask your fishmonger to do this for you).

To prepare stuffing: Chop the soft roes. Place in a bowl and mix with the parsley, onion, crushed clove of garlic, bread crumbs and chopped hard boiled egg. Bind together with a little milk and season well.

Wash and dry the herrings. Spread the stuffing over the fish and roll up neatly. Arrange fish in an oven-proof dish and bake in preheated oven 190C, 375F, Gas Mark 5 for about 25–30 minutes until cooked through. Serve with sauté or boiled potatoes and tomato sauce.

CRAB MORNEY FLAN

This flan makes a delicious lunch served either with hot vegetables, or cold with salad.
Serves 4–6

1 tin of crab or 225g (8oz) fresh
  crab meat
110g (4oz) mushrooms
3 large tomatoes
Parsley
Short crust pastry to line 20.5cm
  (8") flan tin
35g (1½oz) butter
35g (1½oz) flour
35g (1½oz) cheese
300ml (½ pint) milk
1 small onion, sliced
2 carrots, chopped
1 bay leaf
4 peppercorns
Salt and pepper

Line a 20.5 (8 inch) flan tin with pastry. Put onions and carrots with herbs and seasoning. Add milk and bring to the boil. Simmer for 10 minutes, drain and allow to cool. Lightly fry sliced mushrooms, skinned and sliced tomatoes, and put into the base of a flan. Add crabmeat. Make a sauce with flour, butter and milk and pour over crab. Sprinkle with grated cheese. Bake in preheated oven 180C, 350F, Gas Mark 4–5 for approximately 25 minutes.

MEAT
(beef, pork and lamb)

∽

PAPRIKA GOULASH

1kg (2¼lb) best stewing steak, cut
  into cubes
350g (12oz) onions, sliced finely
1½ tsp paprika pepper
1½ tbsp plain flour
1½ dsp tomato puree
600ml (1 pint) beef stock (or cube)
1 tbsp oil
3 large tomatoes, peeled and sliced
Bouquet garni
1 clove garlic
1 sweet pepper

Heat oil in large pan and brown meat and set aside. Lower heat and add onions and after a few minutes add the paprika. Cook gently for about 2 minutes, then add the flour, puree and stock. Stir until boiling, add the meat, bouquet garni, crushed garlic and seasoning. Cover and simmer in preheated oven 170C, 325F, Gas mark 3 for about 2 hours until meat is tender. Then add the sliced pepper and tomatoes. Simmer a further 3–4 minutes, then serve with a tbsp of sour cream swirled over the dish (optional). Serve with boiled potatoes or noodles.

BACON AND ONION CRUMBLE

Serves 4

225g (8oz) streaky bacon rashers
2 large onions
110g (¼lb) mushrooms
110g (¼lb) tomatoes
Salt and pepper
150ml (¼ pint) vegetable stock
25g (1oz) butter

For the topping:
110g (4oz) plain flour
50g (2oz) butter
50g (2oz) grated Cheddar cheese
Salt and pepper

Trim away rind and cut bacon rashers in halves. Peel and slice onions and mushrooms, including the stems, and slice tomatoes. Arrange in layers in a buttered 600ml–1½ litres (1–2 pint) casserole dish, well seasoning each layer. Pour over the stock and add butter in small pieces, cover with lid and place in centre of a hot oven 200C, 400F, Gas Mark 6 and bake for 1 hour.

Meanwhile prepare the topping. Sift flour and seasoning together, rub in butter and stir in cheese. Remove the lid from casserole and sprinkle the crumble topping over top. Return to the oven, placing on the top shelf this time, and bake for a further 25–30 minutes until nicely crisp and brown. Serve with jacket potato and green vegetable.

PORK CASSEROLE

Serves 6

1kg (2¼lb) fillets or small chops
15 small onions or shallots
6 carrots
225ml (8floz) chicken stock
(chicken cube will do)
110g (4oz) redcurrant jelly
1 tsp chopped sage
Juice of 1 orange

Roll meat in seasoned flour and fry in oil to seal. Remove meat, set aside, and then fry onions and carrots. Return meat to pan, adding stock, redcurrant jelly and chopped sage. Cover and cook for an hour in preheated oven 190C, 375F, Gas Mark 5. When cooked add orange juice and bake for a further 15–20 minutes uncovered. This dish goes well with cooked fluffy rice.

HERBY LAMB CASSEROLE

Serves 4

4 loin lamb chops
1 dsp flour
110g (4oz) mushrooms
5 tbsp stock (or lamb stock cube)
1 onion
4 tbsp white breadcrumbs
1 tbsp chopped parsley
½ tsp mixed herbs
25g (1oz) butter
Salt and pepper

Trim any excess fat from the chops and tuck the ends in neatly. Coat chops with flour and seasoning, and arrange them in the base of a shallow fireproof dish. Trim, wash and slice the mushrooms thinly. Add these to the dish and pour in the stock. Slice the onion finely, mix with breadcrumbs, parsley, herbs and seasoning. Spread evenly over the dish. Dot the surface with the butter. Bake in preheated oven 190C, 375F, Gas Mark 5 for 45–60 minutes.

PARCEL OF PORK WITH CIDER

For each person allow:
1 pork chop, trimmed of surplus
fat
1 cooking apple
2 tbsp cider
Salt and pepper
Fresh sage, chopped

Cut a rectangle of foil measuring 30cm x 38cm (12 inches x 15 inches) for each chop, and butter the foil. Place pork chops on the foil and cover with very thin slices of raw, peeled apple. Sprinkle with salt, pepper and a little chopped sage. Add cider. Parcel each chop lightly in foil and bake in centre of preheated oven 200C, 400F, Gas Mark 6 for 45–60 minutes. Serve with vegetables in season.

CURRIED VEAL

Serves 4–6

450g (1lb) veal
25g (1oz) butter
1 small onion
1 small apple
Salt
Lemon juice
A little milk
300ml (½ pint) chicken or
    vegetable stock
1 dsp curry powder
1 tsp curry paste
½ tbsp flour
2 tbsp coconut
175g (6oz) boiled rice
25g (1oz) sultanas

Soak the coconut with the stock for ½ hour. Chop the apple and onion and place in a pan with butter, curry powder and paste. Fry gently for 20 minutes without browning. Add the flour and gradually the strained stock and seasoning. Stir until boiling and simmer for 20 minutes longer. Add the veal cut into small pieces, and simmer until all is tender. Sultanas should be added about 15 minutes before serving, and lemon juice, milk and seasoning immediately before serving. Serve boiled rice separately or on the dish with curry.

BEEF AND CIDER CASSEROLE

Serves 6–8

1kg (2lb) lean stewing steak,
    cubed
3 garlic cloves (optional)
2 medium onions, chopped
2 large carrots, chopped
2 sticks celery, chopped
225g (8oz) mushrooms, sliced
1 large potato, peeled and sliced
Grated zest of an orange
600ml (1 pint) medium sweet cider
1 tsp marmite
1 tbsp chopped parsley
1 tbsp plain flour
2 tbsp oil

Heat oil in a large pan. Cover meat cubes with flour and brown in hot oil. Remove and keep warm. Add crushed garlic, onions, celery and carrots to pan and cook for 1 minute. Add cider and bring to the boil, then add meat, marmite and potato. Cover and simmer for 20 minutes. Transfer to ovenproof dish and cook for 1 hour in pre-heated oven 170–180C, 325–350F, Gas Mark 3–4. Add mushrooms and zest of orange and cook for a further 12–15 minutes. The potato should thicken the liquid, but you can make it thicker by adding one dsp of corn flour. Garnish with parsley. Serve with mashed potatoes and broccoli.

HERBY MEAT BALLS

Ideal for using up the remains of a joint of meat, it doesn't necessarily have to be beef.

Serves 4–6

350g (12oz) minced beef
¾ breakfast cup of breadcrumbs
1 medium sized egg
Salt and pepper
A good tbsp mixed chopped herbs
450g (1lb) tomatoes or tin
   chopped tomatoes
1 carrot
½ red pepper
½ yellow pepper
1 medium onion

Place mince in a basin and mix with breadcrumbs, egg and chopped herbs. Season well. Form into small balls and set aside.

Tomato sauce:
Prepare the carrot and chop into tiny strips. Chop onion and peppers. Fry these ingredients in a little olive oil. Add tomatoes and season. Add various herbs to this sauce (whatever you have). I find cumin, coriander and paprika (½ tsp of each) and a pinch of cayenne pepper a good combination. Fry meatballs until lightly browned, place in a shallow dish with the sauce, and simmer gently for about 15 minutes. Serve piping hot with jacket potatoes and green vegetables.

BEEF POT ROAST

This dish has a rich dark brown gravy, with the added flavour of the strong red wine and black olives.

Serves 6–8

2kg (4lb) lean topside or
   casseroling beef
50ml (2floz) olive oil
3 large onions, peeled
1 garlic clove
125ml (4floz) strong red wine
10 dried prunes
110g (4oz) mushrooms
110g (4oz) stoned, tinned olives
Salt, pepper and a generous pinch
   of powdered ginger

Rub meat with salt, pepper and ginger. Heat oil in a pan. Slice onions very thinly, crush the garlic

clove. Fry all together until soft and golden. Place prepared meat in a pot-type casserole. Pour all fried pan contents on top, add wine and cook at 140C, 275F, Gas Mark 1 for 2 hours. Cover prunes with hot, strained weak tea, and reduce liquid to 12floz. Add tea, olives and prunes around the cooked meat in pot, cover and cook at the same temperature for another 25–30 minutes. Turn into a serving dish and sprinkle with chopped parsley. Noodles or rice go well with this dish.

CHINESE STYLE ROAST PORK

A colourful dish which has a distinct Chinese flavour, and is guaranteed to impress your dinner guests.

Serves 4–6

1.25kg (2½lb) lean boned and
   rolled loin of pork
1.25cm (½ inch) fresh root ginger,
   peeled and cut into thin strips

For the stuffing:
8 spring onions, finely chopped
½ red pepper, seeded and finely
   chopped
1 clove garlic, crushed
1 tsp oil
110g (4oz) dry breadcrumbs
1 tbsp Hoi-sin sauce

For the glaze:
3 tbsp honey
2 tbsp brown sugar
1 tbsp Hoi-sin sauce
1 tsp ground ginger
1 clove garlic, crushed

Cut slits into the joint and push in slithers of ginger. Weigh the joint and calculate the cooking time. Place joint on a rack in a roasting tin. Open roast in a preheated oven 180C, 350F, Gas Mark 4 for approximately 1–1½ hours until crisp and brown. Meanwhile make the stuffing. Fry the spring onions, red pepper and garlic in the oil for 3–4 minutes until soft. Stir in the breadcrumbs and Hoi-sin sauce and mix. Shape into 6–8 stuffing balls. Place on a baking tray and bake for the last 20 minutes of the cooking time. For the glaze, mix all of the glaze ingredients together. 20 minutes before the end of the cooking time, remove joint from oven and brush with glaze. Return to the oven. Re-glaze the joint 10 minutes later. Serve the joint with the stuffing, stir fry vegetables and new potatoes. Alternatively you can slice the joint thinly and serve in Chinese pancakes drizzled with Hoi-sin sauce and garnished with shredded lettuce and cucumber wedges.

QUICK RAISED PORK PIE

Makes 4 individual pies

350g (12oz) good firm shortcrust
   pastry
450g (1lb) lean minced pork
50g (2oz) minced back rashers of
   bacon
50g (2oz) breadcrumbs
1 medium onion, peeled and
   chopped
A clove of garlic
1 tsp mixed chopped herbs,
   (parsley, sage and thyme)

Grease individual raised pie moulds (a cake tin with a loose spring bottom may be used) and line with pastry. Mix the pork, bacon, breadcrumbs, onion and herbs together with egg yolk and fill pastry. Cut small rounds to go on top of pies and pinch up edges. Decorate with leaves and bake in preheated oven 180C, 350F, Gas Mark 4 for 1½ hours until pastry is crisp and brown and meat is cooked through (test with a skewer). These can be eaten hot or cold, and are easy to take on a picnic.

COTTAGE PIE WITH LEEK AND POTATO TOPPING

Serves 4

450g (1lb) minced lamb (or
   pork/beef)
1 onion, chopped
2 carrots, peeled and chopped
2 tbsp plain flour
300ml (½ pint) chicken stock (or
   chicken stock cube)
1 tbsp tomato puree
1 tbsp dried mixed herbs
Salt and black pepper

Leek and potato topping:
700g (1½lb) potatoes, peeled and
   chopped
2 leeks, sliced
Knob of butter
50g (2oz) Cheddar cheese, grated
Salt and black pepper

Boil the potatoes, until softened, adding leeks 5 minutes before the end of cooking. Meanwhile, dry fry the mince, onion and carrots for 3–4 minutes. Add the flour. Gradually add stock, tomato puree and dried herbs. Bring to the boil and stir until thickened. Season. Transfer to an ovenproof dish. Drain and mash the potatoes and leeks with margarine and half the cheese. Season. Place on top of mince mixture. Sprinkle with remaining cheese. Bake in a preheated oven for 30 minutes until golden. Serve with seasonal green vegetables.

ROAST LAMB WITH MINTY STUFFING BALLS

Serves 4–6

1.25kg (2½lb) lean lamb leg or
   shoulder joint
2 cloves of garlic, sliced
8–10 fresh mint leaves

For the stuffing:
2 medium onions, chopped
1 garlic, crushed
1 tsp oil
110g (4oz) dry breadcrumbs
2 tbsp mint jelly
1 tsp fresh mint, chopped

Cut slits into the joint and push in slivers of garlic and mint leaves. Weigh the joint and calculate cooking time. Place joint on a rack in a roasting tin. Open roast in a preheated oven. Meanwhile make the stuffing; fry the onion and garlic in the oil for 3–4 minutes or until soft. Stir in the remaining ingredients and mix. Shape into 6–8 stuffing balls. Place on a baking tray and bake for the last 20 minutes of cooking time. Serve the joint with stuffing, roast potatoes, carrots and broccoli.

HERBY FAGGOTS

These homemade faggots taste far better than the commercially made frozen ones. I usually double up the quantities of ingredients and make a batch at a time for freezing.

Serves 4

110g (4oz) liver (pig's liver for flavour) finely chopped or minced
110g (4oz) streaky bacon, chopped
1kg (2¼lb) onions, chopped
1 dsp mixed dried herbs, chopped

Fry bacon and onions together in a saucepan for 5 minutes, then add the liver and 300ml (½ pint) water. Simmer for about 15 minutes. Add 3 cupfuls of soaked (in beef stock cube) breadcrumbs. Then add herbs, salt and pepper and mix thoroughly. Put into a well greased baking tin, cut into squares, brushing over each square with fat or oil, and bake in a preheated oven 180C, 350F, Gas Mark 4 for ¾ to one hour. Make a rich gravy with juices from baking tin and serve with mashed potatoes and green vegetable.

PORK WITH PINEAPPLE AND DATE STUFFING

Serves 4–6

1.25kg (2½lb) lean pork joint (rolled loin or leg)

Stuffing:
110g (4oz) fresh breadcrumbs
1 small can pineapple in natural juice, pineapple finely chopped, with juice reserved
25g (1oz) dates, chopped
1 lime, rind and juice reserved

Glaze:
1 tbsp lime marmalade blended with 1 tbsp pineapple juice

Make the stuffing by mixing breadcrumbs, pineapple, dates, lime rind and 4 tbsp reserved lime and pineapple juice to bind it. Use mixture to stuff the joint, roll up, securing with skewers or string and cook in preheated oven 180C, 350F, Gas Mark 4 for 1½–1¾ hours, removing from oven 15 minutes before the end of the cooking time, and brushing with glaze. If you are making stuffing balls, instead of stuffing the joint, then add to pan and return to oven.

Vegetables ribbons:
4 carrots, peeled and cut into ribbons (thin sliver slices)
2 courgettes, topped and tailed and cut into ribbons
1 small celeriac, peeled and cut into ribbons
1 tbsp oil
1 tsp honey
1 tsp lemon juice
Salt and pepper

Toss the vegetables in the oil, honey and lemon juice in a flat roasting tin. Sprinkle with salt and pepper. Roast for about 55 minutes to 1 hour in preheated oven 180C, 350F, Gas Mark 4. This can be done before you cook joint and then set aside, warming up when you are ready to serve the meat.

SAUSAGE AND BACON RISOTTO

This dish can be put together and cooked in just over 20 minutes. Can also be made the day before and reheated again.
Serves 2. (Just double ingredients for extra portions)

4 lean rashers of smoked streaky bacon cut into 2.5cm 1 inch pieces
1 small onion, chopped
150g (5oz) risotto rice
400g (14oz) can chopped tomatoes
200ml (7floz) stock
1 courgette, chopped
1 tsp paprika
Salt and pepper to taste

2 tsp fresh basil, roughly chopped

Dry fry sausage, bacon and onion for 2–3 minutes. Add the rice and all the remaining ingredients. Bring to the boil, cover and simmer for 25 minutes, giving an occasional stir. If too wet remove lid for last 5 minutes. Serve with crusty bread and a mixed green salad.

ROAST LIVER

Serves 4

An unusual dish, but you will be surprised to discover how good roast liver is. Ask your butcher to cut you off a solid piece (lamb or pig's), and get him to slice it in the centre, almost through the whole piece, making a pocket. Stuff this pocket with a mixture of one thin chopped rasher of bacon, and one chopped onion mixing them with sufficient breadcrumbs, and moistening the mixture with one beaten egg and a little water. Add seasoning to taste, then tie a string around the liver to hold it together, lard it with rashers of bacon and bake in preheated oven 180C, 350F, Gas Mark 4, until tender. This should take about 45 minutes. Make a brown gravy with the juices in the baking dish, and serve sliced, with redcurrant jelly, mashed potatoes and spinach. Delicious!

BEEF LENTIL CURRY

Lamb or pork works just as well with this dish.
Serves 4

450g (1lb) lean cubed beef
400g (14oz) can chopped tomatoes
300ml (½ pint) stock
75g (3oz) red or green lentils
1 medium onion, chopped
1 clove garlic, crushed
2 tbsp medium curry paste
1 tbsp tomato puree
175g (6oz) cauliflower, cut into small florets
1 red pepper, seeded and cut into chunks

In a large casserole dish place all the ingredients except the cauliflower and red pepper. Mix well, cover and place in a preheated oven 170C, 325F, Gas Mark 3 for 1–1½ hours until the meat is tender. Stir in the cauliflower and red pepper and return to the oven for 25–30 minutes. Serve with rice, naan bread, seasonal vegetables and chutneys.

BEEF LOAF

This loaf is delicious eaten hot or cold and it freezes well too.

Serves 6

450g (1lb) lean minced beef
50g (2oz) white breadcrumbs
225ml (8floz) milk
1 egg
3 tbsp good quality dripping,
  melted (this is essential for
  flavour)
1 tbsp finely chopped parsley
1 tbsp finely chopped onion
1 dsp tomato puree
Salt and pepper

Mix beef, breadcrumbs, salt and pepper and fat together. Add milk and egg, which has been beaten together. Then add onion and parsley and tomato puree and mix all together thoroughly. Pack into a well-greased (or lined with greaseproof paper) 450g (1lb) tin and bake in a preheated oven 180C, 350F, Gas Mark 4 for 45 minutes, basting from time to time. Serve hot with a spicy tomato sauce; sauté potatoes and creamed cabbage, or cold with jacket potatoes and green salad.

FOR SPICY TOMATO SAUCE:
Place 700g (1½lb) roughly chopped tomatoes in a saucepan with 1 tbsp olive oil, 1 garlic clove, peeled and crushed, 1 tbsp fresh or dried basil, 1 tsp dry mustard. Bring to the boil and simmer for 15 minutes. Add chopped basil, pinch of chilli powder and sugar to taste, salt and pepper. Simmer for a further 5–10 minutes. Then pass through a sieve and reheat before serving. **Leave out the chilli powder if you don't like your sauce too hot!**

PORK AND VEAL PLATE PIE

This is good served either hot or cold. If hot, serve with buttered carrots and spinach. If cold, serve with a green salad and creamy mashed potatoes.

Serves 6–8

450g (1lb) lean pork minced
450g (1lb) lean veal minced
¾ tsp salt
½ tsp dry mustard
½ tsp clove garlic crushed
1 small bay leaf crumbled
¼ tsp dried sage, or ¾ tsp fresh,
  chopped
¼ tsp dried thyme or ¾ tsp fresh,
  chopped
Pastry to line a 25.5cm (10 inch)
  pie plate

Mix together the minced meats with salt, mustard, garlic and bayleaf. Heat a little oil and brown the meat for 3–4 minutes. Cover, reduce heat and simmer over a low heat for about 20 minutes, stirring frequently. Stir in the herbs and add seasoning to taste. Cool and set aside. Roll out just over half the pastry to line the pie plate. Spread the meat mixture evenly on the pastry. Roll out the remaining pastry and lay over the meat. Moisten the edges and seal, make three slits on the top of pastry to allow the steam to escape. Brush pastry with beaten egg and bake in preheated oven 200C, 400F, Gas Mark 6 for 45–50 minutes, or until pastry is golden and crisp.

STEAK AND KIDNEY PIE

Serves 4

*225g (8oz) beef skirt or braising
   steak*
1 sheep's kidney, cored
1 level dsp flour
*175g (6oz) ready to roll flaky
   pastry (or short crust)*
½ tsp salt
¼ tsp pepper
150ml (¼ pint) water
*1 medium onion, chopped very
   finely*
*110g (4oz) button mushrooms,
   cleaned*

Cut steak into 2cm (¾ inch) pieces. Skin kidney and cut into small pieces. Lightly fry onion and mushrooms and set aside. Put flour, salt and pepper on a plate and dip each piece of steak into it, together with the kidney and lightly fry. Then place onions, mushrooms, steak and kidney in a pie dish, add enough water to nearly half fill the pie dish and sprinkle over a beef stock cube. Roll out pastry to the shape of pie dish, 2.5cm (1 inch) larger. Wet the edge of the pie dish with cold water. Cut a strip of pastry off all round and place it on the wet edge of pie dish, turning the cut edge to the outside. Moisten this with water, and put the remainder of the pastry on top. Trim the edges with a sharp knife. Make leaves from remaining pastry and ornament the top of pie. Make 3 incisions in the pastry to let steam escape. Glaze pastry with yolk of egg or milk. Bake in pre-heated oven 200C, 400F, Gas Mark 6 for 20 minutes, then lower heat to 170C, 325F, Gas Mark 3 for a further 30–40 minutes.
Serve with mashed potatoes and creamed cabbage.

BEEF STEAK AND MUSHROOM PUDDING

This is a good dish for those cold winter days, and for those nights when dinner may have to be delayed, and an extra hour's cooking will improve rather than spoil it!
Serves 4–6

*225g (8oz) self-raising wholemeal
   flour*
75g (3oz) shredded suet
900g (2lb) lean stewing steak
1 tsp salt
¼ tsp pepper
1 medium onion, chopped
225g (8oz) mushrooms

Prepare a light dry dough from the flour, suet, salt and pepper, adding just enough cold water to mix. Roll out on a floured working surface and line a greased 1½ litres (2 pint) pudding basin, reserving a portion of the pastry for the top. Cut the steak and cleaned mushrooms into cubes and roll in a mixture of two tbsp wholemeal flour, one tsp salt and a ¼ tsp of pepper together with the chopped onion for flavour. Put the meat mixture into the basin with three-quarters of a cup of cold water, and cover with pastry, pinching edges together. Cover with waxed paper or a pudding cloth, tying securely. Steam for at least 3 hours. Serve with jacket potato and buttered carrots.

STUFFED SAUSAGE ROLL

Serves 4–6

700g (1½lb) sausage meat
1 cup white breadcrumbs
1 medium onion, chopped
1 green apple, chopped
1 tbsp chopped parsley
Salt and pepper to taste

Flatten the sausage meat on a sheet of greased paper to form a long rectangle about 1cm (½ inch) thick. Mix the other ingredients and spread evenly over the meat. Roll up as though you were rolling a Swiss roll, pat it into shape and bake in a fireproof dish in a preheated oven 180C, 350F, Gas Mark 4 for about 45 minutes. Serve with a rich brown gravy or a hot tomato sauce and mixed diced vegetables.

ROAST STUFFED PORK

Serves 4–6

1kg (2¼lb) rolled hind loin of pork

Stuffing:
110g (4oz) pie veal
25g (1oz) smoked streaky bacon
    rashers
50g (2oz) pork sausage meat
50g (2oz) fresh breadcrumbs
1 egg yolk
50g (2oz) chopped apricots
Salt and freshly ground pepper

Trim the pie veal and derind bacon and mince both into a large bowl. Add the sausage meat, apricots, breadcrumbs, egg yolk, salt and pepper and mix well.

Remove the skin from the pork, leaving a thin layer of fat on the meat. Place fat-side down on flat surface and make 2 deep cuts along the length of the loin. Season each cut and spoon on the stuffing, pressing it down firmly. Roll the meat into a roll shape and tie at intervals with string. Put into a roasting tin and roast in preheated oven 200C, 400F, Gas Mark 6 for 35 minutes. Reduce the temperature to 180C, 350F, Gas Mark 4 and cook for a further 25–30 minutes and test with a skewer to see that the juices run clear, when cooked. Serve with roast potatoes, carrots and spinach.

SEVILLE PORK 'POT'

450g (1lb) lean pork, cubed
1 tbsp oil
1 onion, chopped
300ml (½ pint) stock
1 tsp ground cinnamon
1 tsp dried thyme
Salt and black pepper
1 tbsp cornflour
150ml (¼ pint) orange juice
3 tbsp Seville orange marmalade
1 medium orange, sliced
8 small onion (or shallots), peeled

Heat oil in large casserole dish, and fry onions until softened. Add meat to brown. Stir in the stock and spices. Blend the cornflour with the orange juice. Add to the pan with the marmalade. Season, then add the orange slices and small onions. Simmer for approximately 1–1½ hours in preheated oven 180C, 350F, Gas Mark 4. Serve with boiled rice, seasonal vegetables or mixed salad.

POULTRY AND GAME

∽

BARBECUED CHICKEN CASSEROLE

This dish can be prepared the day before, and makes a delicious alternative from the traditional roast chicken with stuffing.

Serves 6

1.5kg (3lb) to 1½kg (3lb5oz)
   roasting chicken, jointed
75g (3oz) flour
2 tsp salt
125ml (4floz) olive oil
1 medium onion, sliced
75g (3oz) celery, chopped
50g (2oz) minced green pepper
225ml (8floz) ketchup
225ml (8floz) water
2 tbsp Worcester sauce
2 tbsp brown sugar
¼ tsp black pepper
1 packet frozen whole kernel corn
   – thawed enough to separate
   (optional)

Add salt to flour and then toss chicken in the flour. Heat oil and fry chicken until golden on all sides. Remove and set aside into a large casserole dish. Pour off all but 2 tbsp of oil from the frying pan. Fry onion until golden brown and tender. Add all the remaining ingredients, pour over chicken and put casserole in fridge. Two hours before required, start heating oven to 180C, 350F, Gas Mark 4 and bake chicken, covered, for 1 hour 25 minutes. Add corn and bake un-covered for a further 30 minutes or until chicken is cooked and fork tender.

SOMERSET CIDER CHICKEN

This is a very old recipe, which was given to me by a friend many years ago. I still use it, and vary it by cooking chicken joints instead of a whole chicken.

Serves 4

1 chicken weighing about 1.5kg
   (3lb)
225g (8oz) pork sausage meat
1 small chopped onion
50g (2oz) chopped mushrooms
150ml (¼ pint) dry cider
450g (1lb) small potatoes
35g (1½oz) dripping (you can use
   oil or butter)

Insert the sausage meat into the neck of the cleaned bird and secure

with a skewer. Sprinkle the bird with seasoned flour. Heat the dripping or oil in a pan, add the onion and cook gently until soft. Cook the chicken in the same pan browning all over, and then place all the ingredients into a casserole. Cover with a well-fitting lid and bake at 180C, 350F, Gas Mark 4 for 1 to 1½ hours, or until golden brown and crisp. Serve with roast potatoes and creamed cabbage.

GOLDEN CRUST CHICKEN JOINTS

These joints can be served hot or cold, and make an ideal meal to take on a picnic lunch.
Serves 4 – allowing one joint per person.

4 chicken joints
Salt and pepper
1 beaten egg
2 x 25g (1oz) packets of unsalted crisps
110g (4oz) very finely grated cheese
25g (1oz) softened butter
½ tsp made mustard

Wipe the chicken joints. Butter a fireproof dish and lay the chicken in it without overlapping. Sprinkle with salt and pepper, and brush the surfaces with egg. Crush the potato crisps finely and blend thoroughly with the cheese, butter and mustard. Press this mixture over the joints, cover the dish and bake at 200C, 400F, Gas Mark 6 for 50–60 minutes. Remove the cover for the last 10 minutes of cooking time.

CHICKEN AND BROCCOLI QUICHE

Serves 4

225g (8oz) short crust pastry
300ml (½ pint) double cream
6 florets of cooked broccoli
110g (4oz) cooked chicken, chopped
110g (4oz) Gruyere cheese, grated
3 small eggs
Seasoning

Beat eggs and cream together and add grated cheese. Cook broccoli in salted water until tender, but firm. Roll out pastry and line quiche base or loose-bottomed tin and prick well. Place chopped chicken and broccoli on the base of quiche, season and then add the egg and cream mixture. Bake in preheated oven 180C, 350F, Gas Mark 4. Serve with jacket potato and green salad.

COLD CHICKEN CURRY

When I am in a hurry this is a quick standby meal to prepare, especially in the summer – I just have to make sure I have all the ingredients to hand. It's ideal too for a buffet party, just double up on the quantity of ingredients, assemble it early on the day of your party, and leave it in the fridge until it is needed.
Serves 4

450g (1lb) cooked chicken or turkey
½ cucumber, peeled and chopped
150g (5oz) yoghurt, natural
50g (2oz) finely chopped mushrooms
50g (2oz) sultanas and 50g (2oz) salted peanuts
1 tbsp Cranberry jelly
2 tbsp fresh orange juice

2 tbsp mild curry powder and ground black pepper

Chop cooked chicken into bite size pieces and place into a serving dish. Combine all other ingredients and mix well with chopped chicken. I usually serve this dish with crusty bread and a selection of salads.

TURKEY WITH A BARBECUE SAUCE

This recipe comes into its own after Christmas when I am thinking up ways to use the remains of the left-over turkey. The sauce is good with all other meats too.

Serves 4

350g (12oz) cooked turkey pieces
25g (1oz) butter
Salt and pepper

For the sauce:
110g (4oz) onions, chopped
1 red pepper and 1 green pepper,
    deseeded and chopped
1 tbsp oil
50g (2oz) soft brown sugar
1 level tbsp corn flour
2 level tbsp mustard (English)
Juice of half a lemon
2 level tbsp tomato puree

300ml (½ pint) water
1 tbsp Worcestershire sauce and
    wine glass of sherry

Heat butter in a large frying pan and lightly fry turkey for a few minutes. Remove from pan and set aside, keeping hot. Gently fry onion and peppers in pan. Mix the rest of the ingredients in a bowl and then pour into frying pan with onions and pepper, bring to the boil. Pour over turkey and serve with boiled or fried rice.

RICH CHICKEN PIE

Serves 6

1 medium sized cooked chicken
2 sliced stalks of celery
1 onion, chopped
1 bay leaf
4 sprigs of parsley, chopped
2 tbsp flour
1/3rd cup milk
2 tsp salt
2 slices of ham, chopped (optional)
225g–275g (8oz–10oz) rich short
    crust pastry

Simmer the chicken in sufficient boiling water to half cover with the salt, onion, parsley, bay leaf, ham and celery until tender. Remove meat from the chicken bones and cut into bite-sized chunks, and set aside, adding chopped ham, in a fireproof dish. Strain the stock and add water, if necessary, to bring the quantity up to 425ml (¾ pint). Blend flour to a smooth cream with the milk and stir it into the stock. Bring to the boil, stir until thick and pour over the chicken in a fireproof dish. Roll out ¾ of the pastry to cover the dish, pricking it well with a fork to allow the steam to escape. Use the remainder of the pastry to decorate the pie with leaves. Serve with green peas and broccoli.

TURKEY BURGERS

Serves 4

450g (1lb) minced turkey
1 medium onion, peeled and
  finely chopped
50g (2oz) fresh wholemeal
  breadcrumbs
2 tbsp fresh parsley, chopped
Zest of half a lemon
1 egg, beaten
Freshly ground black pepper

Bind all the ingredients together seasoning well. Divide mixture into four, and roll each piece into a ball, flattening each one to make a burger. Chill for at least 25 minutes, and then grill the burgers for about 15 minutes, turning once. Serve with homemade chips and a mixed green salad.

TURKEY ROLLS

*This is a very simple dish to prepare, but do not add too much seasoning –
the soup has plenty!*
Serves 4

4 turkey breasts (approximately
  450g (1lb) in weight)

Stuffing:
75g (3oz) white breadcrumbs
2 rashers of chopped streaky
  bacon
Grated lemon rind
1 tbsp chopped parsley
1 level tsp mixed herbs
1 beaten egg
20g (¾oz) butter, for frying
1 medium can of concentrated
  chicken soup
A little chicken stock or milk
Chopped parsley to garnish

Beat each turkey breast to make them thin. Make stuffing by mixing all ingredients and moistening with egg. Spread stuffing on each turkey breast, and roll up, secure with string. Melt butter in large frying pan and fry the turkey rolls quickly until nicely golden brown all over. Remove rolls, add soup to the pan and heat gently adding 2 or 3 tbsp of stock or milk. Pour over rolls and cook in covered casserole in pre-heated oven 170C, 325F, Gas Mark 3 for 25–30 minutes. Before serving, remove strings and scatter with chopped parsley. Serve with jacket potato and spinach.

ROAST DUCK WITH ORANGE SAUCE

This recipe came to me from Canada via a friend of a friend. It's a bit unusual, and you may have doubts about using honey on such a rich flavoured bird (I did!), but I found it gave the bird a lovely brown shiny glaze, and didn't impair the taste of the meat one little bit.

Serves 4–6

One plump 2kg (4lb) duckling
2 small peeled oranges
1 stick of celery
Seasoning
300ml (½ pint) white wine
150ml (¼ pint) orange juice
3 tbsp melted honey

For gravy:
A little wine and orange juice.

Cut up the oranges and celery and season with salt and pepper. Stuff the duck with the oranges and celery. Prick the bird all over and rub with salt, place in a roasting tin and cook in preheated oven 220C, 425F, Gas Mark 7, for 10–15 minutes, then reduce heat to 180C, 350F, Gas Mark 4. Cook for a further 30 minutes and then drain off most of the fat and pour the white wine and orange juice over the bird, basting thoroughly. After cooking a further 15 minutes pour 2 tbsp of melted honey over the bird, and 15 minutes later pour over a further tbsp. Cook for a further 15 minutes; the duck should now have a brown shiny appearance.

For the gravy, skim off the excess fat, add a little more wine and orange juice and boil rapidly for a few minutes, at this stage you can thicken gravy with a little cornflour, if you wish, but I think a thin gravy is best. Serve with new potatoes and green peas.

ROAST APPLE DUCKLING

If the use of honey in the above dish really puts you off, then try this recipe, roasting duckling the Somerset way!

One 1.5kg (3lb) to 2kg (4½lb)
   duckling
3 or 4 small cooking apples
Grated rind of 1 small orange
50g (2oz) butter
Salt and pepper
1 dsp flour
1–2 tbsp single cream

Take the giblets from inside the duckling, and use them to make stock for the gravy. Wipe the bird, sprinkle inside with salt and pepper. Peel and core the apples, place them with the orange rind inside the duckling, adding half the butter. Spread the outside with the remaining butter. Dredge with flour and sprinkle with salt and pepper. Place in a roasting tin and bake at 180C, 350F, Gas Mark 4 for 2 hours. Add potatoes to roast for 1¼ hours. When the duckling is carved, lift out the apples, mash them well with a little redcurrant jelly, stir in the cream to moisten and heat through in a small pan. Orange segments left from the stuffing may be used in a salad to serve with the meal, but I think a green vegetable and roast potatoes goes just as well.

PHEASANT PIE

Pheasants are in season from October 1st until February 1st, and a young plump bird should serve 4 people. You may be lucky enough to have one given to you, but if not, then they are readily available in most butcher's shops and supermarkets when in season.
This pie is good either hot or cold, and it freezes well too.

Serves 4

1 young plump pheasant
225g (8oz) streaky bacon, chopped
110g (4oz) mushrooms, sliced
1 dsp corn flour
A little cold milk
Mixed herbs
Seasoning
225g (8oz) puff pastry
A little dry cider

Joint pheasant, legs, wings and breast, (your butcher will do this for you). Put rest of carcass in a little water and simmer for gravy. Line a pie dish with the chopped bacon and lay pheasant pieces on top. Add mushrooms, herbs and seasoning, and add a little cider. Cover with greased paper or foil and simmer in preheated oven 180C, 350F, Gas Mark 4 for 1 hour. Take out dish and cover with rolled out pastry, brush top with beaten egg, return to oven and cook until golden brown, usually about another ½ hour. Mix cornflour with cold milk and add a cupful of hot stock and allow to thicken. Season to taste. When pie is cooked, lift crust off and add thickened gravy. Goes well with mashed potatoes and braised carrots.

RABBIT PIE

Serves 4

900g (2lb) jointed rabbit
225g (½lb) collar bacon in a piece,
   derinded and chopped
375ml (13floz) stock or water
1–2 onions, peeled and sliced
2 carrots, peeled and sliced
1 bay leaf
Juice of half a lemon
Salt and pepper
25g (1oz) flour
1–2 tbsp freshly chopped parsley
175g (6oz) short crust pastry
1 beaten egg for glazing

Soak rabbit in cold, salted water for about 2 hours, and then drain well. Place in a pan with the bacon, stock, carrots, bay leaf, lemon juice and seasonings. Bring to the boil, cover and simmer for 45–60 minutes until tender. Strain off liquid and thicken with flour blended in a little cold water. Return to the boil, stirring frequently. Adjust seasonings and add parsley. Remove meat from the bones and return with the cooked bacon and vegetables to the sauce. Pour into a pie dish and leave to cool. Roll out pastry larger than top of dish and cut 2 cm (1") strip for the rim of the dish. Dampen rim. Position pastry strip then dampen it. Cover with pastry lid. Press edges firmly together and crimp. Decorate with leaves from pastry trimmings. Brush with beaten egg. Cook in preheated oven 200C, 400F, Gas Mark 6 for 20 minutes, and then reduce heat to 180C, 350F, Gas Mark 4 for a further 15–20 minutes. Serve with creamed, mashed potatoes and green vegetables.

VENISON CASSEROLE

Many supermarkets now sell pre-packed venison, already cut into cubes and ready for use, which is ideal for busy cooks, but if you want to buy it fresh from your butcher, it's in season from late June to January. Large joints of venison are best roasted, but a small amount will make an excellent casserole, and you can halve the amount given in this recipe, according to the number of people you are cooking for.

Serves 6

1.5kg (3lb) Venison (roe deer)
2 tbsp flour
1 onion, chopped
Salt and black pepper
110g (4oz) bacon (in one piece)
150ml (¼ pint) red wine
300ml (½ pint) stock or water
2 tbsp red currant jelly
Bouquet garni
1 tbsp wine vinegar
A little oil

Cut venison into 2.5cm (1 inch) square pieces. Trim rind from bacon and cut into rectangles. Heat oil in frying pan and sauté bacon pieces gently for a few minutes, then place in a casserole dish. Coat the pieces of venison with flour and sauté in bacon fat until well browned. Transfer to casserole. Add wine vinegar, stock or water to frying pan and heat through, stirring in all the bits from the sides of pan. Strain this liquid over venison. Add chopped onion, redcurrant jelly, bouquet garni, red wine, and season well. Cover casserole and cook in preheated oven 170C, 325F, Gas Mark 3 for 2–2½ hours until meat is tender. Thicken juices with a little cornflour in the last 5–10 minutes of cooking. Serve with mashed potatoes and cabbage or boiled rice. This dish can also be cooked the day before and reheated, which I think brings out the flavour and tenderises the meat further

VEGETARIAN DISHES

∽

VEGETARIAN NUT ROAST

Serves 4

110g (4oz) butter
3 medium onions, chopped
3 tbsp thyme
2 tbsp flour
300ml (½ pint) water
225g (8oz) breadcrumbs
2 tbsp lemon juice and zest
Seasoning to taste
225g (8oz) cashew nuts, chopped
225g (8oz) hazelnuts, chopped

Melt the butter in a large frying pan, add chopped onions and cook until softened. Add the thyme and flour followed by the water. Remove from the heat and add the rest of the ingredients. Place in a lightly greased terrine dish and cook in a preheated oven 150C, 300F, Gas Mark 2 for 40–45 minutes. Turn out, slice and serve with a crisp green salad.

NUT WELLINGTON

Serves 4

Pastry:
110g (4oz) butter
225g (8oz) wholemeal flour
2 eggs, beaten (1 for glaze)

Nutmeat:
1 onion, finely chopped
25g (1oz) butter
175g (6oz) pine nuts, ground
50g (2oz) pine nuts, whole
110g (4oz) fresh breadcrumbs
1 egg, beaten
2–3 tbsp milk

Stuffing:
50g (2oz) butter
175g (6oz) breadcrumbs
Juice and rind of ½ lemon
½ tsp marjoram
½ tsp thyme
1–2 tbsp chopped parsley

Pastry: Rub butter into flour, stir in egg and add enough cold water to form a firm dough. Chill in fridge for 1 hour.

Nutmeat: Fry onion in butter till soft. Add remaining ingredients, season, then add beaten egg, and milk to moisten as necessary. Mould into a loaf shape.

Stuffing: Rub butter into breadcrumbs. Mix in remaining ingredients and season. Mould into loaf shape. Roll pastry out to a rectangle; lay stuffing down the centre and press nutmeat on top. Buff edges with beaten egg and bring pastry up to make a parcel. Place on a greased baking tray, join facing down. Decorate with pastry trimmings. Brush with beaten egg. Bake in preheated oven 200C, 400F, Gas Mark 6 for about 1 hour. Serve hot or cold with cranberry sauce.

CAULIFLOWER SURPRISE

1 large cauliflower
1 large onion, peeled and sliced
50g (2oz) butter
2 large tomatoes
25g (1oz) flour
300ml (½ pint) milk
Salt and pepper
175g (6oz) grated Cheddar cheese
4 eggs, separated

Break cauliflower into pieces and cook in boiling salted water for 8 minutes. Sauté onion in 25g (1oz) butter until soft, add chopped tomatoes and cook for 2–3 minutes. Make a sauce with remaining butter, flour and milk, season and add 110g (4oz) cheese. Arrange cauliflower in a gratin dish, cover with onion and tomato mixture, and then coat with sauce. Beat egg whites stiffly and arrange on top of the sauce. Make four pockets for the egg yolks, drop in and sprinkle over the remaining 50g (2oz) cheese and grill or bake in a hot oven until crisp and golden.

VEGETABLE HOTPOT

This makes a thick warming vegetable casserole dish.
Serves 4

2 medium onions
2 large carrots
175g (6oz) mushrooms
A sprig of fresh sage or ½oz if
    dried
50g (2oz) butter
1 medium swede
2 leeks
3 sticks of celery
400g (14oz) tin tomatoes
Salt and pepper

Prepare vegetables and chop into bite sized chunks. Sweat onion, swede, celery and carrot in a large saucepan with butter and seasoning until vegetables soften, taking care not to brown. Add tomatoes, leeks and mushrooms with herbs, and simmer with lid on until vegetables are cooked and all the flavours blended. Add a little vegetable stock if too dry.

MARROW BAKE

Serves 4

350g (12oz) marrow, peeled and
    sliced
175g (6oz) tomatoes, skinned and
    sliced
225g (8oz) onions, peeled and
    sliced
350g (12oz) potatoes, peeled
Salt and freshly ground black
    pepper
225g (8oz) Cheddar cheese, grated

Sauté in a non-stick pan, marrow, tomatoes and onion for 2–3 minutes. Cook potatoes in boiling, salted water for 7 minutes – they will be partly cooked. Drain, cut into 5mm (¼ inch) slices. Arrange layers of vegetables in dish. Sprinkle with cheese and seasoning between each layer, finish with a layer of potatoes and cheese. Bake in preheated oven 180C, 350F, Gas Mark 4 for 25–30 minutes, and then brown top under the grill.

VEGETARIAN LASAGNE

Serves 4–6

25g (1oz) butter
1 onion, chopped
2 cloves garlic, crushed
1 small leek, sliced
2 stalks celery, sliced
2 carrots, sliced
2 courgettes, sliced
2 tbsp plain flour
1 bunch spinach
A little milk
175g (6oz) Cheddar cheese
Salt and pepper
250g (9oz) lasagne, cooked
200g (7oz) natural yoghurt
2 eggs

Melt butter in a large saucepan. Add onion, garlic and leek. Cook until onion is transparent. Add celery, carrots and courgettes. Cover and cook without allowing to colour until celery and carrots are just tender. Add flour and cook until frothy. Remove from heat.

Wash spinach thoroughly and, with only the water clinging to the leaves, cook until tender. Drain, reserving all the liquid. Measure liquid and make up to 250ml (9floz) with milk. Return flour and vegetables to the heat, gradually add the liquid, stirring constantly until mixture boils and thickens. Remove from heat and add 50g (2oz) cheese. Season with pepper and salt to taste and set aside. Place one-third of the lasagne at the bottom of a greased ovenproof dish. Spread with half the vegetable mixture. Repeat layers, finishing with a layer of lasagne. In a bowl lightly beat yoghurt and eggs together. Spread this on top of the lasagne. Sprinkle the remainder of the cheese on top. Cook in preheated oven 180C, 350F, Gas Mark 4 for 25 minutes, until golden and heated through.

VEGETABLE STROGANOFF

Serves 4–6

175g (6oz) onions, chopped
3 sticks celery, chopped
1½ tbsp oil
275g (10oz) button mushrooms,
    cleaned and sliced
175g (6oz) courgettes, chopped
225g (8oz) broccoli florets
425ml (¾ pint) vegetable stock
½ tsp mixed herbs
150ml (¼ pint) double cream
1 tbsp cornflour
150ml (¼ pint) dry white wine
Salt and freshly ground black
    pepper
Chopped parsley to garnish

Heat oil in large frying pan and gently sauté onion, celery and mixed herbs. Add the remaining vegetables and cook for 5 minutes. Add the wine and reduce by half, then add the stock and bring to the boil. Mix the cornflour with the cream and add to the vegetables, mix well, reduce the heat and simmer for 10 minutes, or until the vegetables are just cooked and the sauce has thickened. Pour into a serving dish, sprinkle with chopped parsley and serve with long grain rice.

STUFFED AUBERGINES

3 large aubergines
1½ tbsp oil
2 small courgettes
175g (6oz) button mushrooms,
    cleaned and sliced
2 small leeks, cleaned and sliced
225g (8oz) Cheddar cheese
1½ tbsp horseradish sauce
1 small carton natural yoghurt
Salt and freshly ground black
    pepper
1 tsp mixed dried herbs

Cut the aubergines in half length-ways and score with a sharp knife, criss-cross cuts almost through to the skin. Place cut side up onto a baking tray, or shallow ovenproof dish and bake in a preheated oven 200C, 400F, Gas Mark 6 for 15–20 minutes until nicely browned and softened. Remove from the oven and allow to cool. Lightly fry courgettes, mushrooms and leeks in the heated oil until softened. Add the horseradish sauce, seasoning, herbs, and enough of the yoghurt to bind the ingredients. Scoop the flesh out of the aubergines, and add to the mixture. Replace the aubergines in their dish, fill them with the vegetable mixture. Top with the grated cheese and bake in a preheated hot oven 200C, 400F, Gas Mark 6 for 25–30 minutes until crisp and golden brown.

MUSHROOM TARTS

225g (8oz) flat mushrooms,
    cleaned and sliced
1 large onion, finely chopped
35g (1½oz) butter
50ml (2floz) dry sherry
110g (4oz) ready made puff pastry

Heat butter in frying pan and fry onion gently until soft. Add chopped mushrooms, sherry and freshly ground pepper. Add salt to taste and cook, stirring until mushrooms have reduced in bulk and are fairly dry. Allow mixture to cool. Roll out pastry fairly thinly and cut into 10cm (4 inch) circles. Put into greased patty tins and brush edges with egg wash. Fill with cooked mushroom mixture and bake in preheated oven 230C, 450F, Gas Mark 8 for 20–25 minutes. Sprinkle with chopped parsley and serve hot or warm.

VEGETABLE BURGERS

Serves 3–4

6 carrots, cleaned and finely
chopped
4 small onions, peeled and chopped
225g (8oz) yellow split peas,
soaked and simmered until soft
1 tbsp parsley, chopped
1 clove garlic
Salt and pepper
2 small eggs, beaten
110g (4oz) fine dry bread crumbs
2 tbsp oil

Bring carrots and onions to the boil, then simmer until softened. Drain and mash carrots and onions, add yellow peas, chopped parsley and garlic, binding with beaten egg. Make into round burger shapes and dip in egg and breadcrumbs, then heat oil in large frying pan and fry the burgers until they are crisp and brown. These go well with pureed peas or brussels sprouts and creamed potatoes.

CHEESE AND CELERY PIE

Serves 4

450g (1lb) short crust pastry
225g (8oz) Cheddar cheese,
coarsely grated
3 stalks of celery
1 large carrot
2 small onions, peeled
3 tbsp red pepper, chopped
2 eggs
300ml (½ pint) milk
Celery salt
Garlic salt
Freshly ground black pepper

Line a shallow pie dish with half the pastry. Finely chop the onions, carrot, celery and red peppers, and combine with the cheese. Beat eggs with milk and seasoning, and add to the vegetable mixture. Place all into pie case and cover with the remaining piece of pastry, reserving enough to decorate the top. Seal edges well. Slit top to allow steam to escape and decorate with pastry leaves. Brush with milk and bake in preheated oven 200C, 400F, Gas Mark 6 for 25–30 minutes until the pastry is well cooked and nicely browned. Serve with hot mixed vegetables or a side salad.

Puddings

HOT

Apple Dumplings 119

Orange and Lemon Pudding ... 120

Lemon Curd Sponge Pudding ... 120

Damson Cobbler 120

Gooseberry and Cider Flan 121

Rice and Apricot Pudding 121

Gooseberry Crunch 121

Rhubarb and Banana Pie 122

Autumn Blackberry Pudding ... 122

Christmas Pudding (1) 122

Light Christmas Pudding (2) ... 123

My Quick Christmas Pudding (3) ... 123

Coffee Fudge and Cream Pudding ... 124

Marmalade Pudding 124

Orange Meringue Bake 125

Rhubarb Crumble 125

COLD

Lemon Syllabub Tart 126

Chocolate Chestnut Cream 126

Raspberry Brulee 126

Honeycomb Mould 127

Banana and Honey Cheesecake 127

Orange Flummery 127

Lime Custard Cream 128

Chocolate Mousse 128

Port and Prune Fool 128

Apple Ice Cream 128

Rhubarb Chocolate Cake 129

Toffee Mousse 129

Elderflower Sorbet 129

Chocolate Biscuit Cake 130

Walnut Cream Flan 130

Pineapple Meringue Pie 130

Raspberry Trifle 131

PUDDINGS (HOT)

∽

APPLE DUMPLINGS

Serves 6

For shortcrust pastry:
175g (6oz) butter, chilled and cut into small cubes
350g (12oz) plain flour
½ tsp salt
5 tsp caster sugar
4–6 tbsp chilled water

Put the butter, flour, salt and sugar into a large, chilled bowl. Rub the flour and fat together with your finger-tips until they look like fine breadcrumbs. Pour 2 tbsp of iced water over the mixture all at once, toss together lightly and gather the dough into a ball. If the dough crumbles, just add a little more water until it all adheres together. Dust the pastry with a little flour and wrap in cling film and leave to chill in fridge for about 1 hour before using.

Ingredients to make 6 dumplings:
50g (2oz) butter
50g (2oz) soft brown sugar
2½ tbsp fresh lemon juice
1½ tsp finely grated lemon rind
25g (1oz) currants
¼ ground cinnamon
6 large firm, cooking apples
Water
1 tbsp caster sugar

Preheat oven to 220C, 425F, Gas Mark 7. Grease a large baking tray with 10g (½oz) of the softened butter. Cream the rest of the butter and brown sugar together until light and fluffy. Beat in lemon juice and rind, currants and cinnamon. Set aside.

Roll out half the pastry on a lightly floured surface into a circle about 5mm (¼ inch) thick. Cut the dough into 20.5cm (8 inch) rounds with a sharp pastry wheel or knife, using a small plate as a guide. Roll the remaining half of the pastry into a circle and cut into 20.5cm (8 inch) rounds as before. Peel and core each apple, and pack each cavity tightly with about 5 tsps of the currant mixture. Place the apple in the centre of the pastry round and bring the pastry up round it, twisting the edges tightly together at the top. Arrange dumplings, seam side up, on the baking sheet and bake in the centre of the preheated oven for about 10 minutes, then lower heat to 190C, 375F, Gas Mark 5 and bake dumplings for a further 10–15 minutes, until the apples are almost tender.

Moisten the tops of the dumplings with water, and sprinkle each one with about half a tsp of the sugar. Return to the oven and bake for a further 5–10 minutes until the sugar is glazed and the pastry is golden brown. Serve at once with custard sauce or cream.

ORANGE AND LEMON PUDDING

Serves 4–6

1 small orange
25g (1oz) soft margarine
110g (4oz) caster sugar
2 eggs
35g (1½oz) fresh white
   breadcrumbs
1 tbsp cornflour
1 tbsp lemon juice
300ml (½pt) milk

Grate orange rind and extract juice. Separate eggs. Cream margarine, sugar, orange rind and egg yolks in a bowl until light and fluffy. Stir in breadcrumbs, cornflour, orange juice, lemon juice and milk. Whisk egg white until stiff, but not too dry, and lightly fold into mixture. Pour into a 850ml (1½pt) ovenproof dish and place in a roasting tin containing about 1cm (½ inch) hot water. Bake for approximately 50 minutes in preheated oven 180C, 350F, Gas Mark 4 until golden and well risen. When cooked, the pudding has a sponge top and a fruit flavoured sauce underneath.

LEMON CURD SPONGE PUDDING

Serves 4–6

110g (4oz) butter
110g (4oz) caster sugar
110g (4oz) self-raising flour
½ tsp baking powder
2 eggs
25g (1oz) currants
Lemon curd
A pinch of salt and a little milk

Beat butter and sugar to a cream, add well-beaten eggs and sift in flour, stirring all the time. Add about 2 tbsp milk and beat well. Put about two-thirds of the mixture into a well greased pie dish, then a layer of lemon curd, sprinkle currants over the lemon curd, then the remainder of the mixture. Bake in a preheated oven 180C, 350F, Gas Mark 4 for about 40 minutes.

DAMSON COBBLER

Damsons are one of my favourite fruits, and although their season is short, I try to make this pudding at least twice a year when the fruit is available.

1kg (2lb) damsons
Sugar to taste
225g (8oz) self-raising flour
1 tsp baking powder
25g (1oz) sugar
50g (2oz) butter

Gently stew damsons with a little water until tender. Remove stones and add sugar to sweeten. Pour into a 1½ litre (2 pint) flan dish.

For the topping: Sift flour and baking powder, add sugar and rub in butter. Mix to a soft dough with about 7 tbsp of milk. Roll out dough on a floured surface and cut into rounds about 5cm (2 inch) diameter. Place scones overlapping on puree, starting with a ring of four. Brush with milk and cook near top of oven at 190C, 375F, Gas Mark 5 for about 30 minutes. Serve hot or cold with cream.

GOOSEBERRY AND CIDER FLAN

Serves 4–6

225g (8oz) short crust pastry
2 eggs
25g (1oz) cornflour
25g (1oz) icing sugar
450g (1lb) gooseberries, topped
    and tailed
425ml (¾ pint) sweet cider
50g (2oz) sugar
10g (1oz) chopped almonds

Roll out pastry and line a 20.5cm (8 inch) flan dish. Bake blind in pre-heated oven at 200C, 400F, Gas Mark 6 for 25 minutes, and then cool. Bring the cider to boiling point and add gooseberries. Simmer until cooked, then remove gooseberries and set aside. Top up with cider if needed to 300ml (½ pint). Beat eggs and sugar together, mixing in cornflour. Add the hot cider a little at a time, return to heat and stir until thick and creamy. Arrange gooseberries neatly in the pastry case and pour over the cider custard. Smooth the top and sprinkle with almonds. Cover with sifted icing sugar and brown lightly under a hot grill. Serve hot or cold.

RICE AND APRICOT PUDDING

2 small eggs
50g (2oz) pudding rice
600ml (1 pint) milk
225g (8oz) stewed apricots
1 tbsp apricot jam
3 tbsp caster sugar

Put rice into pan with milk and a pinch of salt. Cook slowly with lid on, stirring occasionally until thick and creamy. Add sugar and jam together with beaten egg yolks. Pour into a buttered pie-dish and cook in preheated oven 180C, 350F, Gas Mark 4 until set. Put the stewed apricots on top of the cooked rice. Beat up the egg whites stiffly, and fold in the two tablespoons of caster sugar. Pile on top of the apricots and return to the oven until slightly brown.

GOOSEBERRY CRUNCH

Serves 4

450g (1lb) gooseberries
2 tbsp water
4 level tbsp sugar

Topping:
50g (2oz) butter
1 tbsp golden syrup
50g (2oz) soft brown sugar
1 level tsp cinnamon
50g (2oz) cornflakes

Cook gooseberries in water and sugar. Place butter, syrup, brown sugar and cinnamon together in a large saucepan. Heat gently, stirring continuously until melted and well mixed. Add cornflakes and stir lightly until they are all coated. Pile evenly on top of gooseberries in an ovenproof dish. Place on a baking sheet and bake for about 30 minutes or until topping is lightly browned and crisp. Serve hot or cold with cream or custard.

RHUBARB AND BANANA PIE

Serves 4

450g (1lb) rhubarb
75g (3oz) sugar
The grated rind of ½ a lemon
4 bananas
1 egg white
50g (2oz) almond flakes
2 tbsp caster sugar

Wash the rhubarb and cut into small lengths, put into a pie-dish and sprinkle with lemon rind and sugar. Peel the bananas, crush and beat to a pulp with the caster sugar; when soft beat in the white of the egg. Continue beating until quite stiff. Spread on the top of rhubarb to form a crust, sprinkle the top with blanched almonds, and bake in preheated oven 180C, 350F, Gas Mark 4 for about 30 minutes. Serve hot with custard or cream.

AUTUMN BLACKBERRY PUDDING

Serves 4–6

2 large eggs, beaten
110g (4oz) butter
110g (4oz) caster sugar
110g (4oz) self-raising flour
1 tsp baking powder
¼ tsp vanilla essence
175g (6oz) blackberries (picked
    over and cleaned)

Cream butter and sugar together. Add eggs, then flour, baking powder and vanilla essence, and beat well together. Place mixture in an ovenproof dish and top with blackberries, making sure there is plenty of room for the pudding to rise. Bake in preheated oven 190C, 375F, Gas Mark 5 for about 1 hour. Delicious served with ice-cream.

CHRISTMAS PUDDING (1)

This recipe is at least 150 years' old, and was given to me by a friend. It makes a dark, solid traditional pudding and keeps extremely well.

900g (2lb) raisins
900g (2lb) currants
450g (1lb) sultanas
450g (1lb) suet from butcher,
    chopped fine (I usually buy
    shredded suet from the
    supermarket)
225g (8oz) candied peel
450g (1lb) dark brown sugar
450g (1lb) plain flour
450g (1lb) breadcrumbs
1 sachet of spice
1 nutmeg, grated
6 eggs

Wine glass or so of brandy
600ml (1 pint) stout or beer

Clean fruit, mix well with all the other ingredients, taking care not to make it too wet. Put into greased basins, cover with greased paper and then a cloth. Boil for at least 6 to 8 hours. Dry well. Do not remove cloths or paper as the suet helps to seal for keeping. Steam or boil for another 4 to 5 hours on Christmas Day.